The Devotional Meeting

The Devotional Meeting

by

Wendi Momen

George Ronald
Oxford

George Ronald, *Publisher*
46 High Street, Kidlington, Oxford OX5 2DN

*A catalogue record for this book is available
from the British Library*

ISBN 0–85398–482–4

Printed and bound in Great Britain by
The Cromwell Press Ltd, Trowbridge, Wilts

Contents

Dedicated to the members of the
National Spiritual Assembly
of the Bahá'ís of the United Kingdom
with whom I have had the bounty of serving
1982–2003

Hugh Adamson, Rita Bartlett, Trevor Finch,
Betty Goode Sabri, Philip Hainsworth, Mary Hardy,
Peter Hulme, Nancy Jordan, Barney Leith,
Charles Macdonald, Kishan Manocha, Ridvan Moqbel,
Simon Mortimore, Jan Mughrabi, Iain Palin,
John Parris, Roger Prentice, Shirin Tahzib,
Carolyn Wade, Rob Weinberg

Introduction

When the Universal House of Justice charged the Bahá'í community with establishing 'devotional meetings, open to all the inhabitants of the locality',[1] Bahá'ís were naturally excited by the prospect. Some communities, of course, had long-established regular devotional meetings that were open to everyone but others found the task a little daunting. We at George Ronald, Publisher, wished to make a contribution to the successful prosecution of the Five Year Plan 2001–6 and to the multiplication of its core activities and it seemed to us that offering information and insights into the nature and practice of devotional meetings might be useful, especially to those individuals and communities that were still hesitating to establish regular devotional gatherings.

The examples of devotional meetings contained herein have been shared by Bahá'ís from all parts of the world, from the Mongolian plateau to North American suburbs, from busy Indian cities to small islands in the Pacific, from African towns to their counterparts in Europe, from hamlets in England to that country's great metropolises. They are provided by isolated believers, pioneers, Local Assemblies serving large communities, youth, families, young couples and veteran Bahá'ís. The great variety of gatherings, their lack of uniformity, the creativity and experimentation that characterize them, the sense of dignity and reverence which they evoke and the diversity of approaches to their every aspect demonstrate their flexibility and capacity to be adapted to and appreciated by large numbers of people from different backgrounds living in varying circumstances. They bear witness to the change of culture called for by the Universal House of Justice and to the efforts that Bahá'ís everywhere are making to reach out to their friends, neighbours and relatives with the teachings of Bahá'u'lláh.

Just as this book was completed the International Teaching Centre issued 'Building Momentum: A Coherent Approach to Growth'.[2] This document analyses the progress of the Five Year Plan and charts the great increase in the number of study circles, children's classes and devotional meetings that has taken place since its launch. According to the International Teaching Centre, the number of devotional gatherings increased by 80 per cent in the period April 2001 to October 2002 and multiplied with 'seeming ease in both rural and urban areas'. As the Universal House of Justice has pointed out,

> Devotional meetings begin to flourish as consciousness of the spiritual dimension of human existence is raised among the believers in an area through institute courses.[3]

The International Teaching Centre noted that

> special endeavours to increase the number of devotional meetings often begin with encouraging believers inspired by their institute course on spiritual life to undertake such meetings on their own. Another approach that has resulted in an expansion in number

previously not contemplated has been to hold devotional gatherings in the homes of non-Bahá'ís, who sometimes organize the meetings themselves.[4]

Furthermore, 75 per cent of national communities report that of those who are attending devotional meetings, 20 per cent are non-Bahá'ís.[5] This encouraging development is to be applauded and is a tribute to the devotion, courage and magnificent efforts of Bahá'ís around the world. Surely many of those who now attend devotional meetings and are touched by the spiritual power they find there will want to align themselves ever more closely with the teachings of Bahá'u'lláh, the Manifestation of God for this day.

It is our hope at George Ronald that Bahá'ís everywhere will gain inspiration from these pages and by the experiences of their fellow Bahá'ís in establishing this core activity of our Faith, that they will be encouraged to hold their own devotional meetings and that, as a result, ever greater numbers will enter the Faith of Bahá'u'lláh.

Acknowledgements

Many people from many parts of the world participated in the creation of this book. My thanks to all of them for so generously giving of their time and for sharing their experiences: Mahnaz Afshin, Panchgani, India; Roberta Al-Salihi, Lamin, The Gambia; Robin Bell, Marshall Islands; Don Blanks, Vava'u, Tonga; Soheyla and Sohrab Bolouri, Nukualofa, Tonga; Guitty Bonner, Great Whittington, Northumberland, England; León E. Díaz, Piedras Negras, Mexico; Linda and Duane Dye, California, USA; Amelia Farahbakhsh, Fort McMurray, Alberta, Canada; Mahchid Fatio, Nyon, Switzerland; Judith Fienieg, Lambeth, London, England; Bobbie Guffey, Dayton, Ohio, USA; Corinne Hainsworth, Moscow, Russia; Katherine and Michael Hainsworth, Sevenoaks, Kent, England; Dicy Hall, Sydney, Australia; Dr Charles Hamburger, The Netherlands; Ian Hamilton, Ireland; Dini Hilbron, The Netherlands; Allen Tyrone Johnson, Dayton, Ohio, USA; Vafa Kouchekzadeh, Bournemouth, England; Lois Lambert, Ulaanbaatar, Mongolia; Erica Leith, Abingdon, Oxfordshire, England; Melody Logue, Dayton, Ohio, USA; Semira Manaseki and Ian Holland, Ulaanbaatar, Mongolia; Anne and Stephen Maund, Mynydd Isa, Mold, Wales; Val and Tony McGinley, Tralee, County Kerry, Ireland; Dr A. K. Merchant, Delhi, India; Ephrat Miller, Denvilles,

Havant, England; Dr Moojan Momen, Northill, Bedfordshire, England; Eileen Norman, Rancho Cucamonga, California, USA; Mehry Robiati, Milan, Italy; Mary Sarooshi, Kensington and Chelsea, London, England; Sarah Seagraves, Dayton, Ohio, USA; Doraisamy Suppiah, Malaysia; Amelia Taeed, The Netherlands; Daniel Pierce, Tahiti; Joanna Tahzib-Thomas, Zeist, The Netherlands; Enoch Tanyi, Yaoundé, Cameroon; Steve Thompson, Stoke on Trent, England; Marga van Luijtelaar-Martens, The Hague, The Netherlands; Gary Villiers-Stuart, Northumberland, England; Arthur Weinberg, Canterbury, Kent, England; Robert Weinberg, Lambeth, London, England; Rose Wendel, Dayton, Ohio, USA; Ladan Wise, Alice Springs, Australia; Karen Worth, Howick, KwaZulu Natal, South Africa; Farhan Yazdani, Tahiti; and Amy Youssefian, Kensington and Chelsea, London, England.

I am also grateful to the National Spiritual Assembly of the Bahá'ís of the United Kingdom for permission to reprint material from the website called <www.tranquillity-zone.org.uk> and draw to the attention of readers that the name Tranquillity Zone is trademarked. I would also like to thank the National Spiritual Assembly of the United Kingdom and the editor of the *Bahá'í Journal UK* for permission to reprint articles first published there.

The passage in appendix 3 from Farid ud-Din Attar, *The Conference of the Birds*, translated and with an introduction by Afkham Darbandi and Dick Davis, published in London in 1988, pp. 172–3, copyright Afkham Darbandi and Dick Davis, 1984, is reproduced by permission of Penguin Books Ltd.

I

The Devotional Life

Many people recognize that 'the core of religious faith is
that mystical feeling which unites man with God'.[1] To
achieve this, some believe they must remove themselves
from society and spend their time solely in contemplation
and prayer. For some, the devotional life requires the
seclusion of the devotee and his separation from the day-
to-day life of the world.

Bahá'u'lláh prohibits such a lifestyle,[2] encouraging
rather detachment from 'this world and the vanities
thereof',[3] a subtle but important difference. Bahá'ís live
the devotional life but they live it in the world, earning a
livelihood through their work, which is elevated to the
level of worship,[4] and engaging with others to create a
society of justice, unity and peace in which all people can
prosper. Rather than requiring His followers to live in
monasteries or as hermits, Bahá'u'lláh urges, 'Seclude
yourselves in the stronghold of My love.'[5]

Nor are Bahá'ís ascetics:

The Bahá'í Writings encourage detachment from 'this
world and the vanities thereof' since 'attachment' dis-
tracts the individual from awareness of God. This does

not, however, constitute a form of asceticism or imply a rejection of life's pleasures. Bahá'u'lláh explains: Should a man wish to adorn himself with the ornaments of the earth, to wear its apparels, or partake of the benefits it can bestow, no harm can befall him, if he alloweth nothing whatever to intervene between him and God, for God hath ordained every good thing, whether created in the heavens or in the earth, for such of His servants as truly believe in Him. Eat ye, O people, of the good things which God hath allowed you, and deprive not yourselves from His wondrous bounties. Render thanks and praise unto Him, and be of them that are truly thankful.

The standard is one of moderation: In all matters moderation is desirable. If a thing is carried to excess, it will prove a source of evil . . .[6]

While for some the devotional life requires the 'repetitive recitation of divine Names or short, sacred formulae, often derived from scripture',[7] frequent repetition of sacred verses or hours spent in prayer, Bahá'u'lláh requires of His followers a more modest form of worship, one that seeks to uplift the soul, not to burden it:

Recite ye the verses of God every morn and eventide . . . Pride not yourselves on much reading of the verses or on a multitude of pious acts by night and day; for were a man to read a single verse with joy and radiance it would be better for him than to read with lassitude all the Holy Books of God, the Help in Peril, the Self-Subsisting. Read ye the sacred verses in such measure that ye be not overcome by languor and despondency. Lay not upon your souls that which will weary them and weigh them down, but rather what will lighten and uplift them, so that they may soar on the wings of the Divine verses towards the Dawning-place of His manifest signs; this will draw you nearer to God, did ye but comprehend.[8]

In addition, Bahá'ís recognize that while the devotional life depends on worship, it must be linked with action:

Prayer and meditation are very important factors in deepening the spiritual life of the individual, but with them must go also action and example, as these are the tangible result of the former. Both are essential.[9]

Shoghi Effendi emphasized the relationship between the devotional life and social activity even in his description of the function of the Mashriqu'l-Adhkár:

. . . however inspiring the conception of Bahá'í worship, as witnessed in the central Edifice of this exalted Temple, it cannot be regarded as the sole, nor even the essential, factor in the part which the Mashriqu'l-Adhkár, as designed by Bahá'u'lláh, is destined to play in the organic life of the Bahá'í community. Divorced from the social, humanitarian, educational and scientific pursuits centring around the Dependencies of the Mashriqu'l-Adhkár, Bahá'í worship, however exalted in its conception, however passionate in fervour, can never hope to achieve beyond the meagre and often transitory results produced by the contemplations of the ascetic or the communion of the passive worshipper. It cannot afford lasting satisfaction and benefit to the worshipper himself, much less to humanity in general, unless and until translated and transfused into that dynamic and disinterested service to the cause of humanity which it is the supreme privilege of the Dependencies of the Mashriqu'l-Adhkár to facilitate and promote. Nor will the exertions, no matter how disinterested and strenuous, of those who within the precincts of the Mashriqu'l-Adhkár will be engaged in administering the affairs of the future Bahá'í Commonwealth, fructify and prosper unless they are brought into close and daily communion with those spiritual agencies centring in and radiating from the central Shrine of the Mashriqu'l-Adhkár. Nothing short of direct and constant interaction between the spiritual forces emanating from this House of Worship centring in the heart of the Mashriqu'l-Adhkár, and the energies consciously displayed by those who administer its affairs in their service to humanity can possibly provide the necessary agency capable of removing the ills that have so long and so grievously afflicted humanity.[10]

Thus Bahá'ís pray, meditate and fast whilst they live in the wider community and engage in its activities but they live in it in the 'prayerful state':

Be always in a prayerful state and appreciate the value of everything. Entertain high ideals and stimulate your intellectual and constructive forces.[11]

For a Bahá'í, the goal of the devotional life is clear:

. . . the ultimate aim in life of every soul should be to attain spiritual excellence – to win the good pleasure of God. The true spiritual station of any soul is known only to God.[12]

To achieve such a state, 'to attain spiritual excellence', one must grow spiritually. The requisites for individual spiritual growth have been summarized by the Universal House of Justice:

1. The recital each day of one of the Obligatory Prayers with pure-hearted devotion.
2. The regular reading of the Sacred Scriptures, specifically at least each morning and evening, with reverence, attention and thought.
3. Prayerful meditation on the teachings, so that we may understand them more deeply, fulfil them more faithfully, and convey them more accurately to others.
4. Striving every day to bring our behaviour more into accordance with the high standards that are set forth in the teachings.
5. Teaching the Cause of God.
6. Selfless service in the work of the Cause and in the carrying on of our trade or profession.[13]

In addition, in 1999 the Universal House of Justice decided that it was 'timely for the Bahá'ís in every land to take to their hearts'[14] Bahá'u'lláh's injunction in the Kitáb-i-Aqdas:

It hath been ordained that every believer in God, the Lord of Judgement, shall, each day, having washed his hands and then his face, seat himself and, turning unto God, repeat 'Alláh-u-Abhá' ninety-five times. Such was the decree of the Maker of the Heavens when, with majesty and power, He established Himself upon the thrones of His Names.[15]

'Let all', the Supreme Body urged, 'experience the spiritual enrichment brought to their souls by this simple act of worshipful meditation.'[16] At the same time it took the step of making binding on all believers 'all elements of the laws dealing with obligatory prayers and fasting'.[17]

The Universal House of Justice noted that these spiritual practices are carried out individually:

It is striking how private and personal the most fundamental spiritual exercises of prayer and meditation are in the Faith. Bahá'ís do, of course, have meetings for devotions, as in the Mashriqu'l-Adhkár or at Nineteen Day Feast, but the daily obligatory prayers are ordained to be said in the privacy of one's chamber, and meditation on the Teachings is, likewise, a private individual activity, not a form of group therapy . . .[18]

So important is the spiritual development of the individual that the Universal House of Justice set as one of the objectives of the Six Year Plan 1986–1992 'greater attention to universal participation and the spiritual enrichment of individual believers'. Among the suggestions for goals to fulfil this objective was to 'encourage, where feasible, the practice of dawn prayer'.[19]

However, in addition to the spiritualization of the individual, the community at large needs to develop a more spiritual nature, to incline itself towards God, to develop its own devotional life. The harshness, frivolity and danger of daily life for many people is well known and need not be rehearsed here. The Universal House of Justice has remarked on the 'spiritual aridity' of society, particularly in Europe.[20] A main purpose of the Bahá'í Faith, of the coming of Bahá'u'lláh, is to revolutionize society, to take it from its present level to a higher one, one which is more equitable and is based on justice and love and in which virtues such as honesty and trustworthiness underpin government and drive social activity. Ultimately, humanity as a whole must recognize the Manifestation of God for this age, Bahá'u'lláh, and begin to function under His guidance. Yet humanity will only gradually come to this point and before it is fully achieved there are many stages through which it will pass. The full spiritualization of the planet will, Shoghi Effendi says, occur only after the establishment of the Lesser Peace –

> . . . this consummation will, by its very nature, be a gradual process, and must, as Bahá'u'lláh has Himself anticipated, lead at first to the establishment of that Lesser Peace which the nations of the earth . . . will themselves establish. This momentous and historic step, involving the reconstruction of mankind, as the result of the universal recognition of its oneness and wholeness, will bring in its wake the spiritualization of the masses, consequent to the recognition of the character, and the acknowledgment of the claims, of the Faith of Bahá'u'lláh – the essential condition to that ultimate fusion of all races, creeds, classes, and nations which must signalize the emergence of His New World Order.[21]

– and will precede the Most Great Peace, 'a peace that must inevitably follow as the practical consequence of the spiritualization of the world and the fusion of all its races, creeds, classes and nations'.[22]

It appears that this process of the spiritualization of humanity will begin with the individual and within the Bahá'í community itself. In 1982 the Universal House of

Justice noted that in Europe 'we have not, as yet, found the secret of setting aglow the hearts of great numbers of Europeans with the divine fire'.[23] It 'called upon the Continental Board of Counsellors and the National Spiritual Assemblies of Europe to launch together'[24] 'such a campaign of spiritualization of the Bahá'í community . . . as has never been witnessed' in that continent.[25]

The effect of this is far-reaching. 'Abdu'l-Bahá explained how through devotional gatherings, a city, even a whole country, may become spiritualized:

> Hold meetings and read and chant the heavenly teachings, so that city may be illumined with the light of reality and that country become a veritable paradise by the strength of the Holy Spirit, for this cycle is the cycle of the Glorious Lord and the melody of oneness and solidarity of the world of mankind must reach the ears of the East and West.[26]

Thus the devotional life of the individual and of the wider community are intertwined, just as the spiritual advancement of the individual and the progress of humanity are connected one with the other.

The Devotional Life of the Bahá'í Community

The devotional life of the Bahá'í community finds its genesis in Bahá'u'lláh's institution of the Mashriqu'l-Adhkár.

The Mashriqu'l-Adhkár

Bahá'u'lláh established the Mashriqu'l-Adhkár in His Most Holy Book:

> Blessed is he who, at the hour of dawn,[1] centring his thoughts on God, occupied with His remembrance, and supplicating His forgiveness, directeth his steps to the Mashriqu'l-Adhkár and, entering therein, seateth himself in silence to listen to the verses of God, the Sovereign, the Mighty, the All-Praised. Say: The Mashriqu'l-Adhkár is each and every building which hath been erected in cities and villages for the celebration of My praise. Such is the name by which it hath been designated before the throne of glory, were ye of those who understand.[2]

Here we have a picture of a community of people rising early and, before beginning a day of work, schooling or caring for others, coming together in the Mashriqu'l-Adhkár to turn towards God and listen to the recitation of the holy scripture. How different from our present world of hurrying and busyness! The administrators of the Bahá'í community itself will begin their working day in the Mashriqu'l-Adhkár:

> From the Mashriqu'l-Adhkár, ordained as a house of worship by Bahá'u'lláh in the Kitáb-i-Aqdas, the representatives of Bahá'í communities, both local and national, together with the members of their respective committees, will, as they gather daily within its walls at the hour of dawn, derive the necessary inspiration that will enable them to discharge, in the course of their day-to-day exertions in the Ḥaẓíratu'l-Quds – the scene of their administrative activities – their duties and responsibilities as befits the chosen stewards of His Faith.[3]

'Mashriqu'l-Adhkár' means 'dawning-place of the praises or remembrances or mention of God'. It is 'a complex which, as it unfolds in the future, will comprise in addition to the House of Worship a number of dependencies dedicated to social, humanitarian, educational, and scientific pursuits'.[4] A 'House of Worship forms the central edifice of the Mashriqu'l-Adhkár' which is 'dedicated to the praise of God'.[5] Bahá'u'lláh enjoins the 'people of the world' to 'build . . . houses of worship throughout the lands in the name of Him Who is the Lord of all religions' and to 'make them as perfect as is possible in the world of being, and adorn them with that which befitteth them, not with images and effigies'.[6] While the term 'Mashriqu'l-Adhkár' usually refers to this complex, it is 'also used to refer to any building or room which is reserved for devotions; devotional meetings, particularly dawn prayers; and the heart of the sincere worshipper'.[7] For example, 'Abdu'l-Bahá explains:

> It befitteth the friends to hold a gathering, a meeting, where they shall glorify God and fix their hearts upon Him, and read and recite the Holy Writings of the Blessed Beauty – may my soul be the ransom of His lovers! The lights of the All-Glorious Realm, the rays of the Supreme Horizon, will be cast upon such bright assemblages, for these are none other than the Mashriqu'l-Adhkárs, the Dawning-Points of God's Remembrance, which must, at the direction of the Most Exalted Pen, be established in every hamlet and city . . . These spiritual gatherings must be held with the utmost purity and consecration, so that from the site itself, and its earth and the air about it, one will inhale the fragrant breathings of the Holy Spirit.[8]

We begin to see, then, how the germ of the Mashriqu'l-Adhkár is found in the devotional meeting.

The 'central edifice' of the Mashriqu'l-Adhkár, the House of Worship, is the 'spiritual heart of the community'.[9] From it flows the spiritual energy that enables a community to meet its physical needs:

> Then, gradually, as the outward expression of this spiritual heart, the various dependencies, those 'institutions of social service as shall afford relief to the suffering, sustenance to the poor, shelter to the wayfarer, solace to the bereaved, and education to the ignorant' are erected and function.[10]

'The principle', the House of Justice asserts, is that 'the spiritual precedes the material. First comes the illumination of hearts and minds by the Revelation of Bahá'u'lláh, and then the grass roots stirring of the believers wishing to apply these teachings to the daily life of their community.'[11] 'This process begins in an embryonic way long before a Bahá'í community reaches the stage of building its own Mashriqu'l-Adhkár . . .'[12] Thus even before a House of Worship and its social institutions are erected, the establishment of the spiritual heart of the community is an important step in its development. This the devotional gathering provides.

> Whensoever a company of people shall gather in a meeting place, shall engage in glorifying God, and shall speak with one another of the mysteries of God, beyond any doubt the breathings of the Holy Spirit will blow gently over them, and each shall receive a share thereof.[13]

Dawn Prayers

> Occupy thyself in remembrance of the Beauty of Him Who is the Unconstrained at early morn, and seek communion with Him at the hour of dawn. O 'Alí! Remembrance of Me is a healing medicine to the souls and a light to the hearts of men.[14]

As we have seen, Bahá'u'lláh envisioned people coming to the Mashriqu'l-Adhkár at dawn to begin their day in praise of God. In its Naw-Rúz message of 1974 the Universal House of Justice asked the Bahá'ís to consider holding gatherings for dawn prayers:

One of the characteristics of Bahá'í society will be the gathering of the believers each day during the hours between dawn and two hours after sunrise to listen to the reading and chanting of the Holy Word. In many communities at the present time, especially in rural ones, such gatherings would fit naturally into the pattern of the friends' daily life, and where this is the case it would do much to foster the unity of the Local community and deepen the friends' knowledge of the Teachings if such gatherings could be organized by the Local Spiritual Assembly on a regular basis. Attendance at these gatherings is not to be obligatory, but we hope that the friends will more and more be drawn to take part in them. This is a goal which can be attained gradually.[15]

A year later, in its assessment of the progress of the Five Year Plan, the House of Justice commented to National Spiritual Assemblies that the practice of dawn prayers was becoming widespread:

We have been watching with profound interest the manner in which the goal of encouraging the friends to meet for dawn prayers is being carried out. In some rural areas this has become already an established practice of the friends and indeed a source of blessing and benefit to them as they pursue their activities during the day, as well as increasing the consciousness of community solidarity. In other areas, the friends have found that, because of the distances involved, better results are obtained by meeting for prayer in smaller groups. In yet other areas, as a first step, plans have been made to meet for dawn prayers once a week.[16]

Thus communal dawn prayers provide an opportunity

for the believers to plant the seed of the Mashriqu'l-Adhkár in their communities.

Devotional Meetings

> . . . public meetings in which one day during the week the believers gather to be engaged in the commemoration of God, to read Communes and deliver effective speeches is acceptable and beloved.[17]

Having encouraged the believers to establish dawn prayers as one element of the devotional life of the community, the Universal House of Justice described the further steps that would need to be taken to enable Bahá'í communities to thrive:

> . . . the flourishing of the community, especially at the local level, demands a significant enhancement in patterns of behaviour: those patterns by which the collective expression of the virtues of the individual members and the functioning of the Spiritual Assembly are manifest in the unity and fellowship of the community and the dynamism of its activity and growth. This calls for the integration of the component elements – adults, youth and children – in spiritual, social, educational and administrative activities; and their engagement in local plans of teaching and development. It implies a collective will and sense of purpose to perpetuate the Spiritual Assembly through annual elections. It involves the practice of collective worship of God. Hence, it is essential to the spiritual life of the community that the friends hold regular devotional meetings in local Bahá'í centres, where available, or elsewhere, including the homes of believers.[18]

The importance of devotional gatherings was reiterated a few years later but with the additional guidance that they should not be restricted to members of the Bahá'í community:

> The spiritual growth generated by individual devotions is reinforced by loving association among the friends in every locality, by worship as a community and by service to the Faith and to one's fellow human beings. These communal aspects of the godly life relate to the law of the Mashriqu'l-Adhkár which appears in the Kitáb-i-Aqdas. Although the time has not come for the building of local Mashriqu'l-Adhkárs, the holding of regular meetings for worship open to all and the involvement of Bahá'í communities in projects of humanitarian service are expressions of this element of Bahá'í life and a further step in the implementation of the Law of God.[19]

In 2001 the devotional meeting open to all people became a goal to be achieved by every Bahá'í community:

> Among the initial goals for every community should be the establishment of study circles, children's classes, and devotional meetings, open to all the inhabitants of the locality.[20]

Thus a primary aim of the Bahá'í Faith is facilitated through the establishment of devotional meetings:

> It is a closely-knit and harmoniously functioning community, a world-wide spiritual fraternity which seeks to reform the world first and foremost by bringing about a deep inner spiritual change in the heart of individuals.[21]

3

What is a Devotional Meeting?

Many people ask, 'What is a devotional meeting?' One simple answer comes from the writings of Bahá'u'lláh:

Gather ye together with the utmost joy and fellowship and recite the verses revealed by the merciful Lord. By so doing the doors to true knowledge will be opened to your inner beings, and ye will then feel your souls endowed with steadfastness and your hearts filled with radiant joy.[1]

'Abdu'l-Bahá provides a meltingly beautiful description:

Whatever meeting is held to celebrate the memory of the Abhá Beauty and to listen to the recital of the divine utterances is indeed a rose-garden of the Kingdom; that gathering is strengthened by the reviving breaths of holiness that waft from the unseen world, inasmuch as the outpourings of divine grace are the light of that gathering and in it the effulgent splendours of His mercy are made manifest. I beseech God that those radiant faces may be enabled to shine resplendent in the assemblage of the realm of holiness and that those enraptured beings may be gathered together in the heaven of His mercifulness, that they may chant the verses of divine unity amidst the celestial concourse, sing the melody of His praise and glorification in the Abhá Kingdom, raise the voice of jubilation in the realm on high and the cry of exultation and ecstasy in the Abhá Paradise.[2]

Many of one's friends will no doubt be attracted to a small devotional gathering:

As we have such wonderful prayers and meditations in our writings, the reading of these with friends who are interested in and crave for this type of small meeting is often a step towards attracting them to the Faith. Perhaps you could start such an activity in your city.[3]

It might be held in one's own home:

We hear that thou hast in mind to embellish thy house from time to time with a meeting of Bahá'ís, where some among them will engage in glorifying the All-Glorious Lord . . . Know that shouldst thou bring this about, that house of earth will become a house of heaven, and that fabric of stone a congress of the spirit.[4]

We are encouraged to invite the public – indeed, devotional meetings should be 'open to all the inhabitants of the locality':[5]

Let the friends not hesitate to welcome to their observances, even to those of a devotional character, the non-Bahá'í public, many of whom may well be attracted by the prayers and expressions of gratitude of the believers, no less than by the exalted tone of passages from Bahá'í Writings.[6]

We have seen that the devotional meeting is related to the Ma<u>sh</u>riqu'l-A<u>dh</u>kár and guidance given regarding services to take place in the House of Worship may provide insights into the nature of devotional meetings – their simplicity, flexibility, universality, dignity and informality – underscoring the general principle that there are no rigid forms of worship to which Bahá'ís must adhere or practices which they must follow:

> . . . Shoghi Effendi wishes . . . to urge the friends to avoid all forms of rigidity and uniformity in matters of worship . . . The important thing that should always be borne in mind is that with the exception of certain specific obligatory prayers, Bahá'u'lláh has given us no strict or special rulings in matters of worship, whether in the Temple or elsewhere. Prayer is essentially a communion between man and God, and as such transcends all ritualistic forms and formulae.[7]

> As regard [sic] the whole question of the Temple and services held in it: he wishes to emphasize that he is very anxious . . . that no forms, no rituals, no set customs be introduced over and above the bare minimum outlined in the teachings. The nature of these gatherings is for prayer, meditation and the reading of Writings from the Sacred Scriptures of our Faith and other Faiths; there can be one or a number of readers; any Bahá'í chosen, or even, non-Bahá'í, may read. The gatherings should be simple, dignified, and designed to uplift the soul and educate it through hearing the Creative Word.[8]

> Shoghi Effendi would urge . . . that rigidity in the Baha'i service be scrupulously avoided. The more universal and

informal the character of Bahá'í worship in the Temple
the better . . . Prayers revealed by Bahá'u'lláh and the
Master as well as sacred Writings of the Prophets should
be read or chanted as well as hymns based upon Bahá'í
or non-Bahá'í sacred Writings.[9]

As to the reading of prayers or selections from the Sacred
Writings of other religions such readings are permissible,
and indeed from time to time are included in the devotional programmes of Bahá'í Houses of Worship,
demonstrating thereby the universality of our Faith.[10]

In a communication from the Bahá'í World Centre
regarding devotional meetings, the whole of which
appears in appendix 1, many of these points were drawn
to our attention:

• Care should be taken to avoid developing rigid practices and rituals.

• Bahá'ís are encouraged to use the revealed prayers of
  Bahá'u'lláh and the Báb as well as those of 'Abdu'l-
  Bahá. It is permissible to have prayers and readings
  from the Sacred Scriptures of other religions.

• The form of programme would appear to depend in
  part on the setting, the occasion, and the purposes of
  the gathering.

• The practice of collective worship is one important
  ingredient in the flourishing of community life. It also
  reinforces individual spiritual development.[11]

This provides broad guidance that will enable Bahá'ís and their communities to develop devotional meetings in ways that reflect the diversity, creativity and imagination of the Bahá'ís themselves.

4

Planning Devotional Meetings

Getting Started

Devotional meetings can be as big or as small, as formal or as informal, as simple or as intricate as the host wishes. Whatever the devotional meeting 'looks like', the examples in chapter 8 demonstrate how well-planned and thoughtfully arranged devotional meetings can elate hearts and draw people closer to God. While the organization of such gatherings may appear effortless from the descriptions provided, we all know how much time, effort, energy and resources are involved! This fact alone can make many people think, 'I can't do this!' but a little thought and planning in the beginning will make the process much easier and the outcome enjoyable and uplifting for the hosts as well as for those who attend.

Some of the points below are things you might want to think about before you arrange your first devotional meeting. Deciding the basic 'shape' and size of the gathering may well assist you in making other decisions: if you decide your devotional gathering will be for your family and one or two close friends, you probably will not need to hire a hall or worry about microphones; if you are inviting the mayor and local town councillors, you might not want to ask them to sit on the floor in your family room!

Other points you will decide as you gain personal experience. For example, you may realize that the number of people attending is far greater than you anticipated and that you might want to choose readers and readings in advance, rather than ask people to bring their own; or you may consider that it was not such a great idea to serve refreshments before the devotionals as everyone went to sleep during them as a result! No doubt your devotional meeting will evolve over time with some features added and other aspects abandoned. Also, as we come to learn the value of devotional meetings – their significance to the growth and development of ourselves, our communities and the wider world – we will refine and enhance them to reflect this new learning.

Invitations

The Universal House of Justice has stated that 'Devotional meetings begin to flourish as consciousness of the spiritual dimension of human existence is raised among the believers in an area through institute courses'.[1] Thus you may decide to begin devotional meetings when you have completed the first course of a training institute and many of the people who attend may also come from your study circle.

In addition, you may wish to invite family members who live nearby, neighbours, people you work with, people who provide services for you such as the post lady, the doctor, your children's schoolteachers, the local shopkeeper, and those who have already attended Bahá'í functions such as Holy Days and firesides. You might extend an invitation to members of the local interfaith group, women's organization or retirement centre. A personal invitation is usually appreciated and much more likely to elicit a response than a general advertisement directed at no one in particular. However, Bahá'ís do report that they have had good responses from advertisements placed in local newspapers and parish magazines, from card adverts put up in shops and from general invitations posted on the Internet. Many communities have designed innovative invitation brochures or cards which have met with great success. Some even have a dedicated website.

> Bahá'ís from Alaska to Australia, from Ireland to India, have prepared imaginative brochures to attract seekers to their devotional meetings. Family members, neighbours, and even respondents to newspaper advertisements have been joining the Bahá'ís for prayer and readings from the Scriptures, often enhanced by music and followed by refreshments.[2]

Some people are very nervous about inviting others to devotional meetings, particularly if the event is to be held in their own home. Acquiring the courage to set out on a new path, to undertake a new venture, can be difficult. It is certainly easier to invite people to devotional meetings if they have already expressed an interest in the Faith or have come to other Bahá'í events. Try inviting just one or two people at first. If they enjoy the experience, ask them if they would like to invite their own friends. The simplicity, informality and beauty of the devotional meeting is very attractive to those who have a spiritual thirst and you may well be surprised at the enthusiasm with which your invitation is accepted.

When you concentrate your thoughts on realizing that you now belong to Bahá'u'lláh, are His servant whom He loves and will always help, if you ask Him to, and that the great spiritual strength of the Cause of God is behind you for you to draw upon, you will soon see your fears melting away.[3]

The Universal House of Justice points out that as devotional meetings 'are made open to the wider community through a variety of well-conceived and imaginative means, they attract a growing number of seekers, who, more often than not, are eager to attend firesides and join study circles'.[4] Experiment with ways to invite people, with programmes and with venues. Use creative invitations and intriguing programme titles to capture the attention of your audience.

Creating a Beautiful Environment and a Spiritual Atmosphere

It is natural for the heart and spirit to take pleasure and enjoyment in all things that show forth symmetry, harmony, and perfection. For instance: a beautiful house, a well designed garden, a symmetrical line, a graceful motion, a well written book, pleasing garments – in fact, all things that have in themselves grace or beauty are pleasing to the heart and spirit . . . [5]

One of the titles of Bahá'u'lláh is the Blessed Beauty and it is not surprising that beauty holds a high station in the Bahá'í teachings. You will no doubt wish to make your devotional gathering as fulfilling and beautiful an experience as you can so that it reflects the beauty of the holy words that will be recited. Thus you may wish to find ways to engage all the senses during the event, using ideas, artefacts and details drawn from your own culture or you may want to borrow from other cultures to demonstrate the principle of unity in diversity.

For example, you might create an oasis of serenity by playing soft music or recordings of nature sounds (bird song, waves on the sea, etc.) before the programme begins and during the programme itself. A pleasing visual effect can be made by decorating the room with flowers and candles. One person makes a small indoor 'garden' of beautiful stones and small plants, while the Tranquillity Zone uses draperies to give the impression of a tented pavilion. Some perfume the air with orange blossom or attar of roses, incense or aromatic oils, flowers or scented candles – even setting a small pan of water over a hob with a few drops of vanilla essence or cinnamon in it will make a room very fragrant. Soft cushions on the floor can be provided if people are not sitting on chairs and a comfortable temperature should be maintained. One family's devotional begins with the host shaking a few drops of rose water into the hands of each person as he or she enters the room. They later pass around a small dish of stoned dates and tangerine segments for the guests to eat. At some gatherings light refreshments are served before or after the devotions to foster a sense of fellowship.

However, we should not give the impression that these effects are part of the Bahá'í Faith itself or are necessary aspects of every devotional meeting:

When one is praying in private, one may do what one's heart prompts in such matters. However when prayers are read at meetings, care should be taken not to develop rigid practices and rituals.[6]

At some devotional meetings, guests wait in one room and then, together, enter silently a specially prepared room. In other gatherings, especially in private homes, it is difficult to achieve this and the hosts try to create an atmosphere of devotion and stillness so that people sit in quiet meditation or reflection before the programme begins.

The Programme

The reading or reciting of prayers and selections from the holy scriptures is the core of the devotional meeting. What is selected and how the readings are arranged, who reads or recites them, how many will be chosen, whether music will be used, whether silences should occur and how long the programme will be are matters that need to be determined – there are no set patterns that must be followed.

Factors you might want to consider include the people who are coming, their backgrounds and expectations (what languages do they speak? will they appreciate readings from their own religious tradition?), whether there will be young children present (how long can they sit still?), seating arrangements (it is hard to sit on the floor for a long time if you are not used to it), other features of the event (are you serving refreshments later? do you want to include music?), the time and day of the week (a weekday night might suggest a shorter programme), the occasion (is it a regular devotional meeting or a special one for a holy day, which might suggest a particular prayer or reading?).

Bahá'u'lláh, the Báb and 'Abdu'l-Bahá revealed many prayers and passages of a devotional nature and you will surely wish to include some of these in your programme. Indeed, the whole programme may be devised from the Bahá'í scriptures. However, it is also possible to include other scriptures:

Bahá'ís have the bounty of having the prayers revealed by the Manifestations of God, the Báb and Bahá'u'lláh, as well as by 'Abdu'l-Bahá, which guide us in our devotions, but there is no prohibition on the reading of prayers or selections from the Sacred Writings of other religions.[7]

You have asked whether it is permissible for the friends to recite prayers other than those revealed by the Central Figures of our Faith, prefacing your query by citing an instance when a prayer from a different source was chanted at a Bahá'í public meeting. No prohibition has been found in the Bahá'í Writings against the recitation at public gatherings of prayers other than those provided in Bahá'í Scriptures. You are no doubt aware that in devotional programmes at Bahá'í Houses of Worship it is permissible to include scriptures from other revealed religions, which may include prayers.[8]

A sample of a programme including selections of readings from different holy scriptures can be found in appendix 2.

You may decide to have all the readings in your local language or you may wish to include different languages. For example, some devotional meetings incorporate prayers in the languages of the people who attend, who usually very much appreciate having their own culture honoured in this way. Some hosts also like to include chanting in Persian or Arabic, explaining to their friends that these are the words of Bahá'u'lláh in the original language, an experience many people value. Referring to devotional services in the House of Worship, Shoghi Effendi wrote:

> There is no objection to the recital or chanting of prayers in the Oriental language, but there is also no obligation whatsoever of adopting such a form of prayer at any devotional service in the auditorium of the Temple. It should neither be required nor prohibited.[9]

There are different ways of deciding on the prayers and readings for devotional meetings. All the readings can be chosen in advance or people may offer prayers spontaneously. Some hosts select the readings and readers, prepare a programme and hand a copy to everyone who attends, as a small gift for them to take away. Sometimes all the readings and prayers are chosen and read by the hosts themselves. Some hosts choose the readings themselves but assign the readings to people when they arrive. Others ask those who are attending to choose readings from their own holy scriptures and to read them; sometimes a theme is provided, other times the readers bring readings that are special to them. If those who attend have memorized prayers in their study circle, they may be asked to recite them at the devotional meeting. Because Bahá'ís do not have priests or prayer leaders, you might want to consider whether it would give the wrong impression if only one person were to read all the passages. To underscore the Bahá'í teaching of the equality of women and men, you might wish to include both female and male readers; similarly, your readers might reflect the diversity of religious, cultural and ethnic backgrounds. The participation of children may demonstrate the unity of the Bahá'í family and community while also imbuing children with a sense of reverence.

Bahá'ís have formed the habit of reading scriptures and prayers individually in turn, one after the other. However, it is possible to read them in unison and in some cultures this is most appropriate:

> With reference to your query, about the use of several readers in unison, this is permissible provided it does not seem, or become theatrical in the view of your Assembly.[10]

Reading in unison is not the same as congregational prayer:

> You have asked whether it is permissible for the friends to chant a prayer collectively. There is a difference between chanting a prayer collectively and congregational prayer. The latter is a formal prayer usually led by an individual using a prescribed ritual. Congregational prayer in this form is forbidden in the Faith except in the case of the Prayer for the Dead . . . reciting prayers in unison and spontaneously joining in the recitation of the Words of God is not forbidden . . .[11]

You might, therefore, consider having some of the passages read in unison. This can be particularly appreciated by those who come from a religious tradition in which prayers are said collectively.

Some devotional meetings have a period, or several

periods, of silence in which people are encouraged to pray privately, to meditate or to reflect. Soft music may be played during these times or the room may be completely still.

The length of the programme will vary depending on circumstances and what is culturally appropriate. Recall Bahá'u'lláh's advice:

> Read ye the sacred verses in such measure that ye be not overcome by languor and despondency. Lay not upon your souls that which will weary them and weigh them down, but rather what will lighten and uplift them, so that they may soar on the wings of the Divine verses towards the Dawning-place of His manifest signs; this will draw you nearer to God, did ye but comprehend.[12]

If you are using music, be sure to add this into the overall timing of the programme. Music and the arts can be such an important feature of devotional meetings that chapter 5 is devoted to them.

Some people favour short passages to be read or recited, others prefer longer readings. Again, you will no doubt experiment with this and find what is appropriate for your devotional meeting.

Sometimes people from different religious backgrounds expect a collection of money to be made at the end of a devotional meeting and they may offer this. If this is likely to happen, you might want to include a note in the invitation to say that no collection will be taken.

Joy and Reverence

Devotional meetings are joyful occasions:

Gather ye together with the utmost joy and fellowship and recite the verses revealed by the merciful Lord. By so doing the doors to true knowledge will be opened to your inner beings, and ye will then feel your souls endowed with steadfastness and your hearts filled with radiant joy.[13]

Peruse My verses with joy and radiance. Verily they will attract you unto God and will enable you to detach yourselves from aught else save Him. Thus have ye been admonished in God's Holy Writ and in this resplendent Tablet.[14]

At the same time, they are reverent:

They who are the beloved of God, in whatever place they gather and whomsoever they may meet, must evince, in their attitude towards God, and in the manner of their celebration of His praise and glory, such humility and submissiveness that every atom of the dust beneath their feet may attest the depth of their devotion.[15]

. . . whether read, chanted or sung, prayers should be uttered with proper sense of reverence.[16]

Dignity and reverence befitting the occasion should obviously characterize observances of Bahá'í Holy Days by the friends, but this does not mean that cultural traditions which do not contravene Bahá'í principles may not, and cannot, find expression in the local observances and meetings of the friends.[17]

Thus devotional meetings are not solemn occasions which are dull and uninspiring. Rather, they should be a true refreshment to the soul:

> Humour, happiness, joy are characteristics of a true
> Bahá'í life. Frivolity palls and eventually leads to boredom
> and emptiness, but true happiness and joy and humour
> that are parts of a balanced life that includes serious
> thought, compassion and humble servitude to God, are
> characteristics that enrich life and add to its radiance.[18]

Some Practical Considerations

Many devotional meetings are simple affairs arranged in
one's own home with a few friends. The beauty and ele-
gance of the holy scriptures in themselves are enough to
create a serene and spiritual environment which is attractive and pleasing. However, our natural inclination to
show hospitality often urges us to provide more than this
and to take up some of the suggestions for decorating the
room and offering refreshments. Larger gatherings are
generally more complex and require more effort and
resources.

Here are some of the things you may wish to think
about in preparing a devotional meeting:

- Seating: How many people can be accommodated?
  Are you hoping for an intimate gathering or a large
  crowd? You will need appropriate seating for everyone
  and this may limit your invitation list.

- Cost: Invitations, specially printed cards and
  brochures, flowers, candles, decorations, refreshments
  and so on can be expensive. Is the provision of these
  sustainable?

- Safety: If you are using candles, can they be knocked over easily? Will they ignite draperies? Are there children running around or elderly people who may be unsteady on their feet? Are people likely to get caught up in the draperies, fall over cushions on the floor, stumble in dim light, trip on cables?

- Sitting on the floor: Will people think this is strange? In some cultures it is customary to sit on the floor and to sit on furniture might be considered strange.

- People with disabilities: Can people with different physical disabilities take part with dignity? Can they be honoured as guests or will access be a challenge to them?

- Hearing: If music is played during the recital of scriptures, will people with hearing difficulties find it hard to hear? Do you require a microphone in a large hall? If so, are the speakers properly balanced and placed to prevent distortion and reverberation?

- Reading: If you are using dim lights or candles, can people see to read? As people get older, it becomes increasingly difficult for them to read in darkness, even if their eyesight is good. You might need a torch or a candle in a candle holder to help readers see the words clearly. You might print out readings in a large print size, for example 14 or 16 point, to assist them.

- Perfuming the room: Some people are allergic to certain flowers or to perfume or incense. You might need to alert potential guests to the use of scents.

- Will you serve food and drinks and on what scale? Will people come expecting a full meal or is it enough to serve hot drinks and cake or biscuits? If the food is elaborate, will this take you away from participating in the devotions yourself?

- Are children welcome at your devotional meeting? What arrangements have you made for them? Are there readings appropriate for their age? Are they expected to sit still for a long period without relief?

As you gain experience and confidence in holding devotional meetings, many of these considerations will become second nature to you and you will be able increasingly to enjoy the tranquillity and spiritual refreshment you are providing for others.

5

Music and Arts

Arts and the Bahá'í Faith

The arts hold a very high position in the Bahá'í Faith. There are numerous references in the Bahá'í writings to the importance of the arts, and particularly to music, in uplifting the soul and bringing it closer to God. This is not, perhaps, surprising, when we recall that one of the names of God is 'the Fashioner':

> One of the names of God is the Fashioner. He loveth craftsmanship. Therefore any of His servants who manifesteth this attribute is acceptable in the sight of this Wronged One. Craftsmanship is a book among the books of divine sciences, and a treasure among the treasures of His heavenly wisdom. This is a knowledge with meaning, for some of the sciences are brought forth by words and come to an end with words.[1]

It is the creative power of God that has brought the universe into being and enables human artistic endeavours to be realized:

Every word that proceedeth out of the mouth of God is endowed with such potency as can instil new life into every human frame, if ye be of them that comprehend this truth. All the wondrous works ye behold in this world have been manifested through the operation of His supreme and most exalted Will, His wondrous and inflexible Purpose. Through the mere revelation of the word 'Fashioner', issuing forth from His lips and proclaiming His attribute to mankind, such power is released as can generate, through successive ages, all the manifold arts which the hands of man can produce. This, verily, is a certain truth. No sooner is this resplendent word uttered, than its animating energies, stirring within all created things, give birth to the means and instruments whereby such arts can be produced and perfected. All the wondrous achievements ye now witness are the direct consequences of the Revelation of this Name.[2]

As God has given humanity its artistic ability, it is fitting to use the arts to praise God and their use in devotional meetings is apposite. Indeed, there is a symbiotic relationship between the arts and worship. First, arts in themselves are so important that they are raised to the level of worship:

In the Bahá'í Cause arts, sciences and all crafts are (counted as) worship.[3]

In this great dispensation, art (or a profession) is identical with an act of worship and this is a clear text of the Blessed Perfection. Therefore, extreme effort should be made in art . . .[4]

Second, the meditation and reflection that results from a devotional meeting can be the genesis of arts and music and a meeting that incorporates the arts may stimulate further artistic endeavour and be an inspiration to the creativity of those who attend:

O people of Bahá! The source of crafts, sciences and arts is the power of reflection. Make ye every effort that out of this ideal mine there may gleam forth such pearls of wisdom and utterance as will promote the well-being and harmony of all the kindreds of the earth.[5]

This faculty of meditation frees man from the animal nature, discerns the reality of things, puts man in touch with God.
    This faculty brings forth from the invisible plane the sciences and arts. Through the meditative faculty inventions are made possible, colossal undertakings are carried out; through it governments can run smoothly. Through this faculty man enters into the very Kingdom of God.[6]

Third, arts and music can enhance the spiritual atmosphere of devotional meetings and uplift the soul:

Arts, crafts and sciences uplift the world of being, and are conducive to its exaltation.[7]

The art of music is divine and effective. It is the food of the soul and spirit. Through the power of music the spirit of man is uplifted.[8]

O servant of Bahá! Music is regarded as a praiseworthy science at the Threshold of the Almighty, so that thou

mayest chant verses at large gatherings and congrega-
tions in a most wondrous melody and raise such hymns of
praise at the Mashriqu'l-Adhkár as to enrapture the
Concourse on High. By virtue of this, consider how
much the art of music is admired and praised. Try, if
thou canst, to use spiritual melodies, songs and tunes, and
to bring the earthly music into harmony with the celestial
melody. Then thou wilt notice what a great influence
music hath and what heavenly joy and life it conferreth.
Strike up such a melody and tune as to cause the night-
ingales of divine mysteries to be filled with joy and ecstasy.[9]

Music

Of all the arts, music is perhaps one of the easiest to
incorporate into the devotional meeting. Music itself has
a tremendous influence on the spirit:

> We, verily, have made music as a ladder for your souls, a
> means whereby they may be lifted up unto the realm on
> high . . .[10]

Music is one of the important arts. It has a great effect
upon the human spirit. Musical melodies are a certain
something which prove to be accidental upon etheric
vibrations, for voice is nothing but the expression of
vibrations, which, reaching the tympanum, affect the
nerves of hearing. Musical melodies are, therefore, those
peculiar effects produced by, or from, vibration. However,
they have the keenest effect upon the spirit. In sooth,
although music is a material affair, yet its tremendous
effect is spiritual, and its greatest attachment is to the
realm of the spirit . . . the Teachings of God, whether

they be in the form of anthems or communes or prayers, when they are melodiously sung, are most impressive . . . In short, musical melodies form an important role in the associations, or outward and inward characteristics, or qualities of man, for it is the inspirer or motive power of both the material and spiritual susceptibilities. What a motive power it is in all feelings of love! When man is attached to the Love of God, music has a great effect upon him.[11]

It is the music which assists us to affect the human spirit; it is an important means which helps us to communicate with the soul.[12]

. . . in this new age the Manifest Light hath, in His holy Tablets, specifically proclaimed that music, sung or played, is spiritual food for soul and heart.

The musician's art is among those arts worthy of the highest praise, and it moveth the hearts of all who grieve. Wherefore, O thou Shahnáz, play and sing out the holy words of God with wondrous tones in the gatherings of the friends, that the listener may be freed from chains of care and sorrow, and his soul may leap for joy and humble itself in prayer to the realm of Glory.[13]

The sort of music one chooses to use can determine the mood of the devotional meeting:

. . . melodies, though they are material, are connected with the spiritual, therefore, they produce a great effect. A certain kind of melody makes the spirit happy, another kind makes it sad, another excites it to action . . . With whatever purpose you listen to music, that purpose will

be increased. For instance: there will be a concert given
for the poor and unfortunate, and if you go there thinking of the aim, the music will increase your compassion
and generosity.[14]

Similarly, how music will affect the individuals attending
the devotional meeting will depend on what is already in
their hearts:

Whatever is in the heart of man, melody moves and
awakens. If a heart full of good feelings and a pure voice
are joined together, a great effect is produced. For
instance: if there be love in the heart, through melody, it
will increase until its intensity can scarcely be borne; but
if bad thoughts are in the heart, such as hatred, it will
increase and multiply . . . The meaning is that melody
causes whatever feeling is in the heart to increase . . .
Music really awakens the real, natural nature, the individual essence.[15]

Thus the choice of music, if you are using it, is important
and worth spending some time considering in advance.
Many people choose classical music as particularly
appropriate for devotional meetings but many other types
of music have been used with good effect. One group
uses drumming to enhance its gatherings, whilst another
uses Polynesian choral music. An early Tranquillity Zone
offered to the National Spiritual Assembly of the United
Kingdom interspersed readings from the holy scriptures
with robust African music with a strong beat. Spirituality
is not only enhanced by dreamy melodies but can be
roused by a stirring rhythm.

Setting Scripture to Music

Perhaps one of the most effective uses of music at a devotional meeting is singing or chanting of prayers and other scripture. The combination of the verses of God and music is irresistible to the spirit.

> Bahá'u'lláh, in this glorious period has revealed in Holy Tablets that singing and music are the spiritual food of the hearts and souls. In this dispensation, music is one of the arts that is highly approved and is considered to be the cause of the exaltation of sad and desponding hearts.
>
> Therefore . . . set to music the verses and the divine words so that they may be sung with soul-stirring melody in the Assemblies and gatherings, and that the hearts of the listeners may become tumultuous and rise towards the Kingdom of Abhá in supplication and prayer.[16]

The Universal House of Justice even suggested that scriptures set to music be used for the Nineteen Day Feast, owing to the powerful effect of the holy scriptures combined with music:

> . . . songs whose words are the primary Writings of the Báb, Bahá'u'lláh or 'Abdu'l-Bahá are all quite fitting for the devotional portion of the Feast. Indeed, the Persian chants are such songs, out of a different tradition; they are a way of giving music to the holy Word, and each person who chants does it in a way which mirrors his feeling and expression of the Words he is uttering . . . Inasmuch as the spirit of our gathering is so much affected by the tone and quality of our worship, of our

feeling and appreciation of the Word of God for this day, we would hope that you would encourage the most beautiful possible expression of the human spirits in your communities, through music among other modes of feeling.[17]

Interestingly, the Universal House of Justice not only encourages us to set prayers and scripture to music but to sing these in unison:

It is entirely proper to set prayers to music, and the friends are free to sing prayers in unison. Indeed, assuming that the music is appropriate and that the believers do not make a ritual out of it, it is highly praiseworthy for choirs to sing appropriate verses revealed by Bahá'u'lláh and the Master . . .

We would assume also that the friends will always keep in mind that whether read, chanted or sung, prayers should be uttered with a proper sense of reverence.[18]

Thus you might experiment at your devotional meeting with the singing in unison of some of the holy verses, rather than merely reading them.

Hymns and Poems

In addition to holy scripture and prayers set to music, you might also include hymns and poems written by others, a practice that is also appropriate at the Nineteen Day Feast and in the Mashriqu'l-Adhkár:

With regard to your question concerning the use of music in the Nineteen Day Feasts, he wishes you to assure

all the friends that he not only approves of such a practice, but thinks it even advisable that the believers should
make use, in their meetings, of hymns composed by
Bahá'ís themselves, and also of such hymns, poems and
chants as are based on the Holy Words.[19]

Prayers revealed by Bahá'u'lláh and the Master as well as
sacred Writings of the Prophets should be read or
chanted as well as hymns based upon Bahá'í or
non-Bahá'í sacred Writings.[20]

As regards using hymn tunes of other religions there is no
objection to this. As the Guardian once pointed out, we
do not have at this time distinctive music which could be
called Bahá'í, as such a cultural expression is the flower
of the civilization and does not come at the beginning of
a new Revelation.[21]

Some devotional meetings have made good use of poetry
as well as music. 'Abdu'l-Bahá suggests that poetry can
influence the soul:

What is poetry? It is a symmetrical collection of words.
Therefore, they are pleasing through harmony and
rhythm. Poetry is much more effective and complete than
prose. It stirs more deeply, for it is of a finer composition.[22]

Both Bahá'u'lláh and 'Abdu'l-Bahá wrote poetry and you
may wish to include some of their poems in your devotional meeting. The poems of Ṭáhirih, some of which are
translated into English,[23] might be especially appreciated
at devotional meetings.

Some Considerations

In planning the musical element of your devotional meeting you may wish to consider some of the following points:

- Will you be using 'live' music or recorded? If live, do you require the use of microphones? If so, make sure these are set up and tested in advance. Do the musicians require instruments, music stands or other equipment and do you have space for these? An electronic keyboard may not fit into your living room.

- If you are using recorded music, does the equipment work? Can it be begun with minimal fuss? It is very disturbing to one's concentration if the person operating the music player makes a lot of noise changing tapes or CDs.

- Can the music operator see to cue the music? At one devotional meeting lit only by candles, the room was so dark that the person appointed to turn on and off the music could not see the written programme so did not know when to bring in the music and could not see which CD to load. It was fortunate that humour is one of the 'characteristics of a true Bahá'í life',[24] as on that occasion this is what carried us through.

- Can you prevent reverberation? Many meetings are marred by this – in a devotional meeting, reverberation can be most distressing.

- Is the music at the right level? Very loud music played

after a quiet reading can be quite startling – is this the effect you want?

- Many people with hearing difficulties find it hard to hear when music is played in the background while someone is speaking or reading aloud.

- Is the music culturally appropriate?

  . . . the Cause is absolutely universal, and what might seem a beautiful addition to their mode of celebrating a Feast, etc., would perhaps fall on the ears of people of another country as unpleasant sounds – and vice versa.[25]

- If you are not using a whole piece of music fade it away gradually by turning the volume down slowly. If it has natural silences these could be used to terminate the piece. Never stop the music abrupty mid bar.

6

Hospitality

One of the features of Bahá'í life frequently remarked upon by those who encounter the Faith for the first time is the generosity and hospitality provided to them. So important is the offering of courteous hospitality in the Bahá'í teachings that a reference to it is included in one of Bahá'u'lláh's prayers for the departed:

> I testify, O my Lord, that Thou hast enjoined upon men to honour their guest, and he that hath ascended unto Thee hath verily reached Thee and attained Thy Presence. Deal with him then according to Thy grace and bounty! By Thy glory, I know of a certainty that Thou wilt not withhold Thyself from that which Thou hast commanded Thy servants, nor wilt Thou deprive him that hath clung to the cord of Thy bounty and hath ascended to the Dayspring of Thy wealth.[1]

The generous and friendly reception of guests at your devotional meeting will be its hallmark. Shoghi Effendi has indicated that 'it is only through such acts of hospitality that the true spirit of the Cause is manifested'.[2] A significant aspect of the 'true spirit' of the Faith is the understanding and acceptance of the oneness of humanity. The power of this principle should not be underestimated. In many societies still, people of different backgrounds rarely come together, even if the community is ostensibly 'integrated'. Even more unusual is for people of different religious persuasions to worship together. It is characteristic of Bahá'í gatherings that all people are welcome and, indeed, Bahá'ís positively revel in having as diverse a group as possible at their gatherings. The Universal House of Justice has indicated that

> . . . this intermingling of the peoples of the world is vital to the patterns of life that the followers of Bahá'u'lláh are striving to establish and which are destined to provide an example for the rest of humanity to emulate. As the Bahá'í community continues to grow in capacity, it should give increasing attention to bringing together the diverse members of the human race in ever closer association.[3]

Do not be surprised, however, if newcomers find our endeavours a little startling.

You may wish to make every effort to invite to your devotional meetings those who are new to your area, students from abroad or refugees. Such people are often without family or friends nearby so may value meeting new people. They also have much to offer, including their own arts and talents which they may lend to the devotional meeting.

> . . . urge the Bahá'ís, wherever they may be, to devote more attention to the minorities. This is particularly true in places where there are universities where foreign students belonging to the black, yellow and brown races are

studying. In this way, the friends cannot only obey one of the most beautiful principles of our Faith, to show hospitality to the stranger in our midst, but also demonstrate the universality of our Teachings and the true brotherhood that animates us . . . Likewise the friends should carry their friendship and their teachings to other minority groups . . . such as the Italians, the Jews, the Czechs, the Poles, the Russians, etc.[4]

'Abdu'l-Bahá pleaded for people to take a friendly approach to 'foreigners'. His advice seems particularly appropriate now, when 'asylum seekers' have found such a bad press in many countries:

When a man turns his face to God he finds sunshine everywhere. All men are his brothers. Let not conventionality cause you to seem cold and unsympathetic when you meet strange people from other countries. Do not look at them as though you suspected them of being evil-doers, thieves and boors. You think it necessary to be very careful, not to expose yourselves to the risk of making acquaintance with such, possibly, undesirable people.

I ask you not to think only of yourselves. Be kind to the strangers, whether come they from Turkey, Japan, Persia, Russia, China or any other country in the world.

Help to make them feel at home; find out where they are staying, ask if you may render them any service; try to make their lives a little happier.

In this way, even if, sometimes, what you at first suspected should be true, still go out of your way to be kind to them – this kindness will help them to become better.

After all, why should any foreign people be treated as strangers?

Let those who meet you know, without your proclaiming the fact, that you are indeed a Bahá'í.

Put into practice the Teaching of Bahá'u'lláh, that of kindness to all nations. Do not be content with showing friendship in words alone, let your heart burn with loving kindness for all who may cross your path.

Oh, you of the Western nations, be kind to those who come from the Eastern world to sojourn among you. Forget your conventionality when you speak with them; they are not accustomed to it. To Eastern peoples this demeanour seems cold, unfriendly. Rather let your manner be sympathetic. Let it be seen that you are filled with universal love. When you meet a Persian or any other stranger, speak to him as to a friend; if he seems to be lonely try to help him, give him of your willing service; if he be sad console him, if poor succour him, if oppressed rescue him, if in misery comfort him. In so doing you will manifest that not in words only, but in deed and in truth, you think of all men as your brothers.

What profit is there in agreeing that universal friendship is good, and talking of the solidarity of the human race as a grand ideal? Unless these thoughts are translated into the world of action, they are useless.

The wrong in the world continues to exist just because people talk only of their ideals, and do not strive to put them into practice. If actions took the place of words, the world's misery would very soon be changed into comfort.[5]

When thinking of who to invite to our devotional meetings, we might recall 'Abdu'l-Bahá's approach.

Let them call to mind, fearlessly and determinedly, the example and conduct of 'Abdu'l-Bahá while in their midst. Let them remember His courage, His genuine love, His informal and indiscriminating fellowship, His contempt for and impatience of criticism, tempered by His tact and wisdom. Let them revive and perpetuate the memory of those unforgettable and historic episodes and occasions on which He so strikingly demonstrated His keen sense of justice, His spontaneous sympathy for the downtrodden, His ever-abiding sense of the oneness of the human race, His overflowing love for its members . . .[6]

At the same time, we need to be sensible and take reasonable precautions about inviting strangers into our homes. For example, it may not be wise for a lone woman or young person to advertise devotional gatherings in their home unless family or friends will be attending as well.

Another aspect of the hospitality you are offering at the devotional meeting is food and drink. The breaking of bread together as a social activity is an accepted tradition in many cultures and is also a feature of many Bahá'í gatherings, even to the extent that it forms a vital part of the Nineteen Day Feast. However, you will need to decide whether serving food and drink is appropriate, or even possible, at your devotional meeting and, if so, at what scale you are going to provide it. Most people appreciate a hot or cold drink, depending on the weather, after a period of sitting and listening to prayers, and they usually like to have a little something to snack on as well. Depending on your culture and circumstances, this could be as simple as fresh fruit, biscuits or cake, potato crisps or crackers and cheese or a full meal, complete with dessert.

In planning your devotional meetings, do consider whether the provision of food and drink serves or detracts from your purpose. The smell of a cake baking can heighten one's appreciation of scripture or distract one completely. You will not get much out of the devotions yourself if you are struggling with a complicated meal in the kitchen. However, this tranquil picture of a devotional gathering in the home of 'Abdu'l-Bahá hints at how prayers may be complemented by simple refreshments:

Florence waited every day for the little knocking at her door which invited her to morning prayers with the Holy Household.

Reaching their long reception room with its latticed blinds, she would remove her shoes and enter in stocking feet. A gentle breeze blew through the blinds, and beyond them she could see the green vineyards of Mount Carmel, spread out in the morning sun. Alone, at the head of the room on a divan, sat the Greatest Holy Leaf. Regal and yet at the same time self-effacing, she wore the graceful flowing headscarf and garments of the East. Another divan ran the length of the room under the many windows, and at its head, at the right hand upper corner and near His sister, sat 'Abdu'l-Bahá. Halfway down from the Master was His consort, Munírih <u>Kh</u>ánum. Beside her, one of her daughters was chanting prayers of Bahá'u'lláh and verses from the Qur'án. At the further, the 'lower', end of the room were little boys and girls of the Household, and from time to time one or another child would sweetly chant.

Here too were the tall samovars, and quietly moving about, women in Eastern dress were serving hot tea in small glasses placed on saucers. The tea was being unobtrusively served and drunk simultaneously with the prayers. The meeting was not cold and formal – it was natural and easy, more like people gathered as a family to listen to music.[7]

7

The Coherence of the Core Activities

Devotional meetings, valuable as they are in themselves, are also part of a wider programme of change and growth within the worldwide Bahá'í community. For years Bahá'ís struggled to take the Faith to more places around the globe, arising to pioneer to ever more remote regions and, in the process, they spread themselves thinly across many nations. Eventually, the Faith took root in virtually every country in the world and the time had come to 'effect a deeper penetration of the Faith into more and more regions within countries'.[1] The need for more, better equipped, human resources had become acute: if the Faith were to rapidly increase the number of new believers entering into its fold, more of its avowed supporters needed to be deepened, committed, involved participants in the process of bringing people closer to their God. Thus in the Four Year Plan 1996–2000 the Universal House of Justice focused the attention of the Bahá'í world community on the importance of training institutes for enabling change and promoting the entry of troops into the Faith, remarking that 'those who enter the Faith must be integrated into vibrant local communities, characterized by tolerance and love and guided by a strong sense of purpose and collective will'.[2]

The training institute process was 'to endow ever-growing contingents of believers with the spiritual insights, the knowledge, and the skills needed to carry out the many tasks of accelerated expansion and consolidation'.[3] The 'active involvement of the Counsellors and Auxiliary Board members in their operation' was 'essential' if the institutes were to succeed. Thus, as we have seen, in its Riḍván message of 1996 launching the Four Year Plan, the Universal House of Justice declared that 'there should be no delay in establishing permanent institutes designed to provide well-organized, formally conducted programmes of training on a regular schedule'.[4]

Soon training institutes blossomed in every country such that by Riḍván 1998 the House of Justice remarked that

Tens of thousands of individuals have over the last two years completed at least one institute course. The immediate effects upon them have been a greatly strengthened faith, a more conscious spiritual identity, and a deepened commitment to Bahá'í service.[5]

By the close of the Four Year Plan at Riḍván 2000 the Universal House of Justice noted a remarkable change in the worldwide Bahá'í community:

We bow our heads in gratitude to the Lord of Hosts, our hearts brimming with joy, as we witness how marvellous a difference four years have made since the launching of the global Plan now concluded at this Festival of Splendours. So marked was the progress achieved during this period that our world community attained heights from which bright new horizons for its future exploits can clearly be discerned.

The quantitative difference resulted mainly from a more critical qualitative difference. The culture of the Bahá'í community experienced a change. This change is noticeable in the expanded capability, the methodical pattern of functioning and the consequent depth of confidence of the three constituent participants in the Plan – the individual, the institutions and the local community. That is so because the friends concerned themselves more consistently with deepening their knowledge of the divine Teachings and learned much – and this more systematically than before – about how to apply them to promulgating the Cause, to managing their individual and collective activities, and to working with their neighbours. In a word, they entered into a learning mode from which purposeful action was pursued. The chief propellant of this change was the system of training institutes established throughout the world with great rapidity – an accomplishment which, in the field of expansion and consolidation, qualifies as the single greatest legacy of the Four Year Plan.[6]

But although the change in the culture of the Bahá'í community was dramatic, we had come to 'a bridge between times', when 'the capacities developed through a century of struggle and sacrifice by a handful of intoxicated lovers of Bahá'u'lláh' were to be 'applied to the inescapable tasks remaining to the Formative Age'.[7] Thus not only were new training institutes to be formed and the work of existing ones augmented, the House of Justice identified that 'our children need to be nurtured spiritually and integrated into the life of the Cause'.[8] Already, in 1999, the Universal House of Justice had told the Bahá'í community that 'strategies to advance the process of entry by troops' could not 'ignore children and junior youth, if the victories won in one generation' were not to be 'lost with the passage of time'. 'The education of children', the House had said, '. . . requires special emphasis so as to become thoroughly integrated into the process of community development'.[9] Now it called for 'the community as a whole, to show a proper attitude towards children and to take a general interest in their welfare'. The House asked training institutes to be 'certain to include in their programmes the training of teachers of children's classes', appealed to parents 'to give constant attention to the spiritual education of their children', and reminded them that they 'should support Bahá'í children's classes provided by the community'.[10]

To assist parents and Bahá'í communities in their task, in July 2000 the International Teaching Centre issued 'The Spiritual Education of Children and Junior Youth: Bahá'í Classes for Children', a document offering 'suggestions' to 'stimulate consultation in Bahá'í communities on the all-important subject of systematizing Bahá'í children's classes'. Here the Teaching Centre noted how one of the 'limiting factors' in providing children's classes – 'an insufficient number of teachers' – was overcome by the success of training institutes which enabled believers 'to gain a deeper Bahá'í identity, including an awareness of the responsibilities of parents and institutions towards children' and through training 'a larger and larger number of teachers of children's classes'. The training of teachers, the Teaching Centre asserted, 'will remain an ongoing focus of every institute'.

On 9 January 2001 the Universal House of Justice gave to the Conference of the Continental Boards of Counsellors in the Holy Land the blueprint for the Five Year Plan to be launched the next Riḍván. The training institutes so carefully nurtured in the Four Year and the Twelve Month Plans had given the Faith 'a powerful instrument for developing the human resources needed to sustain large-scale expansion and consolidation'.[11] A 'new impetus' had been given to Bahá'í children's classes. In the Five Year Plan, both these initiatives would be expanded, extended and enriched as Bahá'í communities around the world formulated and then executed plans for systematic growth.

A new feature of the Five Year Plan was the planning process itself, 'a spiritual process in which communities and institutions strive to align their pursuits with the Will of God'.[12] Owing to the spread of the Faith and 'increased institutional capacity', it was possible 'to focus attention on smaller geographic areas'.[13] Countries were divided into 'clusters' based on 'culture, language, patterns of transport, infrastructure, and the social and economic life of the inhabitants'.[14] Each cluster could be categorized as to the level of development the Faith had achieved within it. Thus while some clusters were unopened, others had 'strong communities of deepened believers' able to take on the 'challenges of systematic and accelerated expansion and consolidation'. The thrust of the Five Year Plan was for a cluster to move gradually through a series of levels until 'conditions' were 'propitious' for it to establish intensive programmes of growth.[15]

And now the Universal House of Justice brought all the strands together. Systematic programmes of growth, 'far from requiring grandiose and elaborate plans', were to 'focus on a few measures that have proven over the years to be indispensable to large-scale expansion and consolidation'. 'Among the initial goals for every community', the House declared, 'should be the establishment of study circles, children's classes, and devotional meetings, open to all the inhabitants of the locality.'[16] The 'close collaboration' of training institutes, Auxiliary Board members and their assistants and Area Teaching Committees was essential for the implementation of these programmes.

As the Five Year Plan progressed, Bahá'ís and their communities everywhere responded to the appeal of the Universal House of Justice and the symbiotic relationship among all the core activities of the Plan began to be realized. By January 2003 the House of Justice, in reviewing the progress of the Plan, could write:

> In most clusters, movement from one stage of growth to the next is being defined in terms of the multiplication of study circles, devotional meetings and children's classes, and the expansion they engender. Devotional meetings begin to flourish as consciousness of the spiritual dimension of human existence is raised among the believers in an area through institute courses. Children's classes, too, are a natural outgrowth of the training received early in the study of the main sequence. As both activities are made open to the wider community through a variety of well-conceived and imaginative means, they attract a growing number of seekers, who, more often than not, are eager to attend firesides and join study circles. Many go on subsequently to declare their faith in Bahá'u'lláh and, from the outset, view their role in the community as

that of active participants in a dynamic process of growth. Individual and collective exertions in the teaching field intensify correspondingly, further fuelling the process. Established communities are revitalized, and newly formed ones soon gain the privilege of electing their Local Spiritual Assemblies.

The coherence thus achieved through the establishment of study circles, devotional meetings and children's classes provides the initial impulse for growth in a cluster, an impulse that gathers strength as these core activities multiply in number. Campaigns that help a sizeable group of believers advance far enough in the main sequence of courses to perform the necessary acts of service lend impetus to this multiplication of activity.

It is evident, then, that a systematic approach to training has created a way for Bahá'ís to reach out to the surrounding society, share Bahá'u'lláh's message with friends, family, neighbours and co-workers, and expose them to the richness of His teachings. This outward-looking orientation is one of the finest fruits of the grass-roots learning taking place. The pattern of activity that is being established in clusters around the globe constitutes a proven means of accelerating expansion and consolidation. Yet this is only a beginning.[17]

At Riḍván 2003 the Universal House of Justice noted that 'While the world continues on its tumultuous course, the Five Year Plan has reached the operational capacity to enable our community to make giant strides towards its major aim of advancing the process of entry by troops'.[18]

The core activities were central to this achievement.

The institute process has demonstrated even more promi-
nently than before its influence as a generating force for
expansion and consolidation. The core activities of the
Plan have attained a scale far outstripping that of the past
year. As a result, a growing number of friends are now
active in the teaching and administrative work throughout the world, demonstrating the infectious spirit of
confidence inspiring the enthusiasm of their efforts.
Youth and children have been more systematically
involved in the programmes of the community, and
non-Bahá'ís have been participating more numerously in
study circles, devotional meetings and children's classes.
It is indeed heartening to note that, in the brief period
since the beginning of the Plan, where in many communities these three core activities had been sporadic they
have become regular features and have multiplied. Here,
then, is a snapshot of a world community focused and on
the move as never before.[19]

This positive picture was reinforced by the International
Teaching Centre in April 2003:

Nowhere was this 'rise in activity' more evidenced than in
the increase in study circles and other core activities.
According to the data available at the Bahá'í World
Centre, the number of study circles worldwide increased
from 3,600 in April 2001 to almost 9,000 in October
2002. The participation of individuals in devotional gatherings and children's classes increased by 80 and 63 per
cent respectively in the same period, with the highest percentage rise in both categories registered by countries in
Asia. For the most part this proliferation of community
activities was the expression of individual initiative by

believers who translated into action what they had internalized from their training institute courses.[20]

The development of the Faith within clusters is linked with the interlacing of the core activities:

Movement of the cluster toward the next stage of development is directly associated with 'the multiplication of study circles, devotional meetings and children's classes, and the expansion they engender'.[21] As the pool of trained human resources grows, an increase in these and other activities occurs naturally . . . The growing pool of human resources generated by the institute process has made it possible to establish an increasing number of two other core activities: devotional gatherings and children's classes.

It is important to recognize that each of the core activities is intimately linked with the others, that the success of one can be a springboard for the success of the others. Together, these activities empower us to attract people into the Faith. The Teaching Centre noted:

In various parts of the world, special endeavours to increase the number of devotional meetings often begin with encouraging believers inspired by their institute course on spiritual life to undertake such meetings on their own. Another approach that has resulted in an expansion in number previously not contemplated has been to hold devotional gatherings in the homes of non-Bahá'ís, who sometimes organize the meetings themselves . . .

Wherever systematic efforts were made to invite receptive parents who had children in Bahá'í classes or individuals who were attending devotional meetings to join study circles, the results were also encouraging. For these souls, their introduction to the Bahá'í Faith has been first and foremost the Word of God. Connecting the seekers immediately with the Writings of Bahá'u'lláh has been a uniformly effective approach . . .[22]

Thus your decision to hold devotional meetings can be a key to accelerating the process of entry by troops into our much-loved Faith.

8

Examples of Devotional Meetings

In the pages that follow are examples of devotional meetings that have been held in Bahá'í homes and communities around the world. Written by those who have initiated or participated in the gatherings, the essays demonstrate that there is no set form that devotional meetings take and that the possibilities are enormous.

Some of the devotional meetings described here have been long established, others have been arranged only recently. Some take place in villages on tiny islands, others in large metropolitan cities in Western countries. One contribution describes the challenges met by a young family having daily devotionals at home, another about hosting regular gatherings in a capital city. One essay comes from the 'Tranquillity Zone' web page while others describe devotional meetings in the early days of the Faith. Some of the devotionals take place only on special occasions, others weekly. In some the focus is on non-Bahá'í youth; other devotional meetings have only recently become open to all.

Some devotional meetings are arranged around a theme, some around an age group or population. In some the readings are chosen from all the holy scriptures, in others only Bahá'í selections are read. Many use music to enhance the atmosphere, some use other artistic endeavours. All provide inspiration and insights for those of us who wish to begin to hold devotional meetings of our own.

Devotional Meetings in the Early Days of the Faith

Bahá'u'lláh in Baghdád
Shoghi Effendi

Shoghi Effendi describes the effect on the Bábís of Bahá'u'lláh's presence in Baghdád:

The complete transformation which the written and spoken word of Bahá'u'lláh had effected in the outlook and character of His companions was equalled by the burning devotion which His love had kindled in their souls. A passionate zeal and fervour, that rivalled the enthusiasm that had glowed so fiercely in the breasts of the Báb's disciples in their moments of greatest exaltation, had now seized the hearts of the exiles of Baghdád and galvanized their entire beings. 'So inebriated,' Nabíl, describing the fecundity of this tremendously dynamic spiritual revival, has written, 'so carried away was every one by the sweet savours of the Morn of Divine Revelation that, methinks, out of every thorn sprang forth heaps of blossoms, and every seed yielded innumerable harvests.' 'The room of the Most Great House,' that same chronicler has recorded, 'set apart for the reception of Bahá'u'lláh's visitors, though dilapidated, and having long since outgrown its usefulness, vied, through having been trodden by the blessed footsteps of the Well Beloved, with the Most Exalted Paradise. Low-roofed, it yet seemed to reach to the stars, and though it boasted but a single couch, fashioned from the branches of palms, whereon He Who is the King of Names was wont to sit, it drew to itself, even as a load-stone, the hearts of the princes.'

It was this same reception room which, in spite of its rude simplicity, had so charmed the Shujá'u'd-Dawlih that he had expressed to his fellow-princes his intention of building a duplicate of it in his home in Kázimayn. 'He may well succeed,' Bahá'u'lláh is reported to have smilingly remarked when apprised of this intention, 'in reproducing outwardly the exact counterpart of this low-roofed room made of mud and straw with its diminutive garden. What of his ability to open onto it the spiritual doors leading to the hidden worlds of God?' 'I know not how to explain it,' another prince, Zaynu'l-'Abidín Khán, the Fakhru'd-Dawlih, describing the atmosphere which pervaded that reception-room, had affirmed, 'were all the sorrows of the world to be crowded into my heart they would, I feel, all vanish, when in the presence of Bahá'u'lláh. It is as if I had entered Paradise itself.'

The joyous feasts which these companions, despite their extremely modest earnings, continually offered in honour of their Beloved; the gatherings, lasting far into the night, in which they loudly celebrated, with prayers, poetry and song, the praises of the Báb, of Quddús and of Bahá'u'lláh; the fasts they observed; the vigils they kept; the dreams and visions which fired their souls, and which they recounted to each other with feelings of unbounded enthusiasm; the eagerness with which those who served Bahá'u'lláh performed His errands, waited upon His needs, and carried heavy skins of water for His ablutions and other domestic purposes; the acts of imprudence which, in moments of rapture, they occasionally committed; the expressions of wonder and admiration which their words and acts evoked in a populace that had seldom witnessed such demonstrations of religious transport and personal devotion – these, and many others, will forever remain associated with the history of that immortal period, intervening between the birth hour of Bahá'u'lláh's Revelation and its announcement on the eve of His departure from 'Iráq.[1]

The Devotional Meetings of Áqá 'Alíy-i-Qazvíní
From *Memorials of the Faithful* by 'Abdu'l-Bahá

'Abdu'l-Bahá describes one of the early believers and the devotional meetings he held:

This eminent man had high ambitions and aims. He was to a supreme degree constant, loyal and firmly rooted in his faith, and he was among the earliest and greatest of the believers. At the very dawn of the new Day of Guidance he became enamoured of the Báb and began to teach. From morning till dark he worked at his craft, and almost every night he entertained the friends at supper. Being host in this way to friends in the spirit, he guided many seekers to the Faith, attracting them with the melody of the love of God. He was amazingly constant, energetic, and persevering.

Then the perfume-laden air began to stir from over the gardens of the All-Glorious, and he caught fire from the newly kindled flame. His illusions and fancies were

burned away and he arose to proclaim the Cause of
Bahá'u'lláh. Every night there was a meeting, a gathering
that rivalled the flowers in their beds. The verses were
read, the prayers chanted, the good news of the greatest
of Advents was shared. He spent most of his time in
showing kindness to friend and stranger alike; he was a
magnanimous being, with open hand and heart.[2]

Family Worship

Many families hold daily devotional meetings in their own
homes. These are probably the simplest and perhaps most
usual type of devotional meeting. Sometimes members of
the Bahá'í community, neighbours or other friends participate. Often these are held early in the morning before
the parents leave for work and the children go to school,
following this guidance of 'Abdu'l-Bahá:

> Every day at first light, ye gather the Bahá'í children
> together and teach them the communes and prayers.
> This is a most praiseworthy act, and bringeth joy to the
> children's hearts: that they should, at every morn, turn
> their faces toward the Kingdom and make mention of
> the Lord and praise His Name, and in the sweetest of
> voices, chant and recite.[3]

Bahá'u'lláh Himself urges us:

> Teach your children the verses revealed from the heaven
> of majesty and power, so that, in most melodious tones,
> they may recite the Tablets of the All-Merciful in the
> alcoves within the Mashriqu'l-Adhkárs.[4]

Amatu'l-Bahá Rúḥíyyíh <u>Kh</u>ánum tells of the devotional gatherings in the home of 'Abdu'l-Bahá:

> In those days of Shoghi Effendi's childhood it was the custom to rise about dawn and spend the first hour of the day in the Master's room, where prayers were said and the family all had breakfast with Him. The children sat on the floor, their legs folded under them, their arms folded across their breasts, in great respect; when asked they would chant for 'Abdu'l-Bahá; there was no shouting or unseemly conduct.[5]

One family describes its own experiences with morning family worship:

> When our children were very small, we always used to say prayers with them after reading stories and before they went to sleep. We usually recited the same prayers every night for a long period and in this way they learned quite a few prayers over the years. But when they became older, they didn't want us to read stories to them anymore or to listen to their prayers. So in consultation we decided to try morning prayers instead. The children would say their prayers privately at night but in the morning we would say prayers together as a family.
>
> Well, that was the idea! Getting the children up a little bit earlier in the morning proved something of a task. With only one bathroom in the house, it was hard to get everyone in and out quickly. We are definitely not a 'morning' family and there was a fair amount of grumbling at the earliness of the hour. We had the usual rush around to collect gym shoes and lost homework and to find misplaced keys. The pressure to leave the house on

time so as not to miss the school run was enormous and our attempts to say prayers in the interval between a hurried breakfast and piling into the car were not very successful. Everyone was so disgruntled that after a week or two we consulted about whether or not we should continue the experiment.

At the family consultation it was agreed that we should persevere but perhaps have the prayers first, then do everything else. We also thought it might be an idea to choose the prayers the night before and set out the prayer books.

So this is what we did. Every evening each of us chose a prayer and one person also selected a passage from the Bahá'í scriptures. Eventually we decided to read a paragraph or two a day from a book such as *Gleanings* until the book was finished. We sometimes chose music to start. Then in the morning, as soon as we all woke up, we came together in the living room, played the music, said the prayers and read a paragraph from the writings. After that everyone went to wash up, dress, eat breakfast and gather all the paraphernalia for the day before setting off for school and work. Somehow, this seemed to give us more time and a feeling of peace and calm rather than rushing.

Here is the experience of the Tanyi family in Cameroon:

In my home, the programme consists solely of prayers. There is no music. We have not yet started inviting non-Bahá'ís. We have only invited Bahá'ís, and apart from a Bahá'í who lives nearby, all the participants are members of my family – five of us. We hold these devotional meetings once every Friday evening at home and we feel they are successful. But I wish to see it as a more lively activity, with prayer, the reading of a few devotional or inspiring passages from the writings, soul-touching or moving music, perhaps accompanied with some hand clapping and gentle body-swaying.

What makes us hesitate is the fear that our neighbours might label the Faith a sect if we give the devotional meetings the flavour of some Christian denomination, and the fear of our being labelled as pastors. The major obstacle is our personality. At the moment we are too timid to open up, sing and dance – not rock'n'roll, of course! In Cameroon a sect is a cult associated with black magic, human sacrifice, etc. It is, therefore, a highly derogatory description. But we are hoping to find a way to invite people. We would like to see devotional meetings held at dawn or first thing early in the morning. Some soul-stirring religious music, Bahá'í or non-Bahá'í, would precede or follow the prayers and would reflect the theme of the prayers.

African Experiences

Monthly Devotionals in Lamin, The Gambia
Roberta Al-Salihi

Lamin is a village in the Gambia, a small riverine country in West Africa. Formerly a British colony, the Gambia gained independence in 1965. The first Bahá'í arrived in February 1954 and by 1975 the Faith had grown so extensively that a National Spiritual Assembly was elected.

The Local Spiritual Assembly and the local Bahá'í community of Lamin Village decided in September 2002 to hold monthly devotional gatherings in order to respond fully to the guidance of the Universal House of Justice to promote the three core activities: children's classes, study circles and devotional gatherings. The weekly children's classes have been going on for 20 years, the study circle intermittently for two years and the devotional gatherings since October 2002.

The devotional gathering was also felt to address the need to share prayers and readings with people of all faiths and with local religious leaders following the distribution of the Universal House of Justice's letter to the world's religious leaders. Members of the Gambia Christian Council and local Islamic teachers (Ustas) were particularly included in the invitations to the public to join us for prayers and readings from the Bible, the Qur'án and the Bahá'í writings.

The 45-minute long devotional gatherings start with recorded music of Bahá'í holy writings and comprise selections from all the holy books read by all willing participants on the theme of peace and unity. Languages used include English, Arabic and Mandinka. While attendance is small, each gathering is slightly larger than the one before. The venue is the home of a Bahá'í family.

In accordance with the clustering and categorization goals of the Five Year Plan, Lamin is now working with neighbouring Banjulnding Bahá'í community to have a joint devotional programme.

Spiritual Break
Karen Worth

Howick is a town in KwaZulu Natal, South Africa. Before the Five Year Plan, the majority of devotional meetings in the area were directed primarily at Bahá'ís:

Bahá'ís gathered, read from the writings, had tea and went home. Occasionally a seeker would attend. When the Universal House of Justice asked for an increase in devotional meetings, a young mother decided to change this pattern:

I recently started a devotional meeting on the second Sunday morning of each month in my home. It is by formal invitation only – an artist friend of mine, not yet a Bahá'í, designed the invitations (she is also attending a study circle). I came up with a list of all of my friends who have shown interest in the Faith since we moved to Howick and have also included spiritually-minded friends. I have invited two or three Bahá'ís, hand-picked. The response has been very good, with my contacts bringing their friends now.

I have not named the devotions but just ask people to come to a devotional meeting. I choose all the readings myself. Each month has a theme and incorporates writings from the various religious holy books. Music is played in the background while I and another Bahá'í read the short quotations. There is time in between (two to three minutes) for contemplation. The devotional meeting is very similar to what I understand a Tranquillity Zone to be like.

The chairs are set in a circle, with a small kist in the centre with candles and flowers on it. I often burn incense before my guests arrive. Curtains and windows are open.

I serve a light tea and muffins after the formal programme. On the tea table I have pamphlets available together with small collections of the writings for the guests to take away.

Most of my friends see this as a spiritual break and therefore people do not bring children to the devotions. However, they are welcome to bring children along, as my husband Steve takes all the kids for an outing so that the space is not interrupted.

These devotional meetings are new for this area but I am very hopeful. I am using it to seed my study circles and also to draw my reluctant-to-join-a-religion friends closer to the Faith.

American Experiences

Reuniones Devocionales
León E. Díaz

In the border city of Piedras Negras, in northeastern Mexico, the small Bahá'í community currently holds two devotional gatherings (*reuniones devocionales*), open to everyone interested in joining people of different beliefs in a common worship of the one God in a spirit of true brotherhood and love. Since attendance is still very small, ranging from three to 12 participants, we have a basic yet very effective programme. The participants sit in a circle. The hosts passes around Bahá'í prayer books for those wishing to read from them. Then we ask the attendees what would they each like to pray for. This step is very important because each person gets to offer his or her supplications to God on a particular issue, ranging from personal affairs such as jobs, health, difficulties and plans, to family matters, to world issues. At the same time, everyone participates, respectfully and reverently, in praying for everyone else's needs. Thus, every individual feels he or she has prayed for everyone in the meeting and that everyone else has prayed for him or her. The feeling is that of friendly thankfulness and love towards one another.

After everyone has prayed 'enough' (sometimes one round is enough, sometimes we feel moved and inspired to complete several rounds), someone offers a spiritually uplifting story and we include a few Bahá'í songs to end. Throughout the meeting, soft classical music can be heard in the background.

An interesting feature occasionally occurs when we have visitors from a Christian background coming for the first time. They will often feel inclined to recite prayers from their church or an excerpt from the Bible but, little by little, as they continue to return, they begin reading from the Bahá'í prayers and then they end up using them in every meeting. They somehow feel this is respectful to the Bahá'í hosts, while also recognizing the tremendous force and beauty of the prayers revealed by the Central Figures of our Faith. Occasionally we are honoured by visitors from other communities and our gathering is enhanced by the beauty of prayers recited in Spanish, English, Persian, Arabic or French.

The people are invited in different ways. We publish invitations in local newspapers and have a monthly campaign to invite people door-to-door to children's classes and devotional gatherings. We also invite people we come across on the street, on a bus or inside a store. Sometimes when we begin a conversation with a complete stranger, he or she just happens to be a Bahá'í!

The devotional gatherings are held every Monday and Tuesday evenings, in two different areas of the city. One has been functioning for about a year or so, while the second is very new. They are both held in Bahá'í homes.

Those who attend are from different backgrounds. Several are seekers; some are friends or relatives of individual Bahá'ís; some are Bahá'ís, of course! And everyone is encouraged to bring their children along.

Both gatherings are successful despite the relatively low number of participants. Many of those who attend are intrigued and have asked if they can host similar meetings in their homes. Also, through these devotional meetings people have become interested in learning more about the nature of prayer and our relationship with our Creator. Some have ended up participating in a study circle using Ruhi Institute book 1 or have their children attend a children's class.

Sacred Place
Amelia Farahbakhsh

Fort McMurray, Alberta, Canada, has a Bahá'í community of about 50. As part of an individual initiative, it held the first of its devotional gatherings over a year ago.

I believe that all of us need a time when we can escape from our busy lives and go on a spiritual and sacred journey. I personally enjoy organizing these events because I get energized spiritually through helping participants to have a relaxing and inspirational experience.

We offer this time for people to relax in a pleasant, uplifting environment in which they can enjoy inspirational music and spiritual writings. This is a very simple process and those who attend can choose to participate in different ways: by sitting back and savouring the music and the readings or by reading their own prayers during the periods of personal prayer and meditation which are available in the middle of the programme.

The event is advertised in the local newspaper, attracting seekers to every meeting. The programme includes meditative and inspirational music together with readings from Bahá'í and other religious scriptures on various topics.

Everyone is invited for 7:30 p.m. We book two rooms, one as a waiting room, the other for the actual devotional room, which we call 'Sacred Place'. We usually start preparing the devotional room with candles, flowers, wall decorations, lighting and so on about an hour ahead of the programme. As people gather in the waiting room, a printed programme is given to them. At 7:30 everyone is invited into the Sacred Place.

The music that accompanies the programme includes various pieces selected earlier and recorded on a CD. After a brief welcome, the programme starts and continues for about 50 minutes, uninterrupted. Afterwards participants have the opportunity to enjoy refreshments and to socialize.

The devotional gatherings have been a success and have attracted between one and five seekers to each of the monthly meetings.

Spiritual Connections: An Interfaith Experience: An outreach programme sponsored by the Spiritual Assembly of the Bahá'ís of Rancho Cucamonga, California
Eileen Norman

A group of women, sponsored by the Spiritual Assembly of Cucamonga, formed a group called 'Women on the Move', whose purpose is 'to take vital and meaningful steps towards the emergence of a peaceful society through action-oriented programmes of community service and awareness-raising which will help improve the status of women around the world and most urgently in our own communities'.

In connection with this effort, Women on the Move began a series of devotional meetings, entitled 'Spiritual Connections'. These are held monthly in a community centre and regularly attract between 30 and 40 attendees, about half of them not Bahá'ís.

The meetings are advertised in the newspaper and through individual mailings and the invitations state that they are 'open to people of all faiths, with readings from the holy books of all religions'.

The programme usually consists of four or five readings, each about a page in length. The readers are both Bahá'í and non-Bahá'í and they are informed ahead of time of what they will be reading. The readings are followed by a talk of about 20 minutes on a virtue, chosen in advance and given to the speaker as the topic. The speakers are either Bahá'ís or non-Bahá'ís. For example, a Bahá'í speaker who was a journalist spoke on 'Integrity in Journalism' while a minister from a nearby Unitarian Church spoke about honesty.

Refreshments are then served. An effort is made to make this a beautiful display of cakes and fruit that is pleasing to the eye.

The entire programme, including refreshments, lasts one and a half hours.

Music in Dayton
Bobbie Guffey and Sarah Seagraves

Music plays a major role in many devotional meetings.

Here is one in which music takes centre stage.

Approximately four years ago one of the Bahá'ís volunteered to coordinate Sunday morning devotions. Several months after the devotions began an Auxiliary Board member from Fort Wayne, Indiana, met with our Local Spiritual Assembly and shared with us a number of programmes in which we were being encouraged by our National Teaching Committee to participate.

At the next Assembly meeting it was decided to concentrate on developing our devotional meetings, teaching and enhancing the Feast. Devotions are held every other Sunday at our local Bahá'í Centre from 12:30 p.m. to approximately 2:00 p.m. When devotions first started we invited speakers who spoke on a variety of subjects of their choosing. Music and prayers were used to augment the service. Then another Bahá'í found prepared devotional topics on the American National Bahá'í website.

We have been using this format for some time now and we feel the devotions are successful. We have combined appropriate music of all types and we now have a youth to assist with this. We use 'Bahá'í' music, rap, country and western, traditional, Christian and classical. We also sing hymns. We even have several members of a Bahá'í choir in Dayton who occasionally sing at our devotions. It has been interesting to watch the reaction of some of the older Bahá'ís to the unfamiliar music but when they listen to the words they enjoy the different beats. We know that to continue our success we have to reach all ages.

When we began, there were as few as two to three Bahá'ís present but devotions have grown so much that we now fill the room. Attendance is consistent but there have also been many visitors. Our Assembly likes to think that this period has been useful in deepening the community in 'how to hold effective and spiritually uplifting devotions'. We now have plans to go into the wider community surrounding the Centre with invitations to 'our neighbours' to attend devotions. We also have plans to place a 'Welcome to Devotions' banner in front of the Centre. Our goal is: 'Reaching out to our neighbours, diversity in all aspects, with love and understanding'.

Consistency is important. At least one of the original organizers attends every devotional meeting. For this to succeed we know that it takes dedication to the project.

Prayers in the Park
Vafa Kouchekzadeh

Peace is an important issue for Brazilians. It is easy to get them interested in anything that will promote peace, so they were attracted to devotional meetings on this theme.

In the centre of Brasilia, the capital of Brazil, is a large, beautiful, peaceful park. Many go there to enjoy the trees and the flowers and the birdsong and the park is usually full of people, especially at the weekends. One of the Bahá'ís thought it might be possible to have Bahá'í activities in the park. The idea caught the imagination of the youth, who decided to host devotional meetings there.

Between three and five Bahá'í youth set up a tent in the park every Sunday morning. Near the tent they arrange a number of fold-out stools and a table. They have ready a cassette tape recorder, tapes of classical music and batteries, as well as prayer books, the scriptures of different religions and copies of prayers which have been printed out nicely. The youth then go around the park meeting people and inviting them to prayers for peace at the tent. They offer everyone a leaflet containing a few Bahá'í prayers. Each leaflet has a tear-off section which people can send in to obtain a small Bahá'í prayer book. Because the prayer book is free, quite a lot of people take the leaflet and later send in the tear-off slip.

The youth hold at least three devotionals at the tent during the Sunday morning and a number of people participate each time. Although the general theme is peace, there is no set programme and those who attend are encouraged to read from the prayers and scriptures provided or to say a prayer from their own religious tradition. Sometimes music is played on the cassette recorder but because the music does not always carry well in the open, the youth have had to be flexible about its use. At the end of the devotional the people are invited to attend other Bahá'í activities.

The devotional gatherings at the tent are quite popular and people sometimes ask for special prayers to be said for them or their loved ones. For example, one woman whose son had recently passed away approached the youth and asked that one session be devoted to saying prayers in his memory. The flexibility of the programme made this possible. The woman was so touched by the beauty of the devotional meeting that she attended many other times.

Asian and Indian Experiences

Mongolian Devotionals
Semira Manaseki and Lois Lambert

Mongolians are a very spiritual people and prayer is one of the aspects of the Bahá'í way of life that really attracts many to the Faith. In the Mongolian version of Tibetan Buddhism, prayer is normally an activity confined to monks and lamas and a small number of qualified individuals. Others may ask these individuals to pray for them. It is a matter of real pleasure for a Mongolian to discover the Bahá'í prayers and to be able to pray themselves for their loved ones and for spiritual progress. Many people who are not Bahá'ís own and treasure their Bahá'í prayer books.

In Mongolia the Day Star Centre of Learning has been operating since 1996 and the systematic training of human resources through the Ruhi Institute courses (books 1–7) is well established. Throughout the country there are many friends who have completed all the books in the existing series of courses and those who have completed book 7 are recognized as trained facilitators for all the preceding books. Their activities are coordinated by the Day Star Centre of Learning. Since the commencement of the Five Year Plan there has been a focus on the three core activities of study circles, devotional gatherings and children's classes and there have been many campaigns throughout the country to increase the number of Bahá'ís and others who are interested to join study circles and take part in devotional gatherings. Most people declare their faith in Bahá'u'lláh during their study of Ruhi books 1 and 2. As book 1 focuses on the importance of prayer and devotionals, participants are encouraged to set themselves goals of holding a growing number of devotional gatherings in their own homes or visiting the homes of their friends and neighbours, whenever appropriate or possible. Offering to read prayers with a sick neighbour or with a family that has a particular challenge to overcome, as well as offering prayers of joy and thanksgiving is accepted gratefully and with enthusiasm in Mongolia and all these are recognized as devotional gatherings. A prayer book is a treasured gift.

In addition, more formal devotional gatherings are held regularly in the community. The Mongolian Bahá'í community has for many years been respected for its very beautifully arranged public devotional gatherings to commemorate special days such as World Religion Day, United Nations Day and the UN Vigil for Peace, to which representatives of all religions and prominent people are invited. In the capital, formal gatherings are held in each of the six clusters of Ulaanbaatar. Each cluster collects reports on the number of devotional gatherings held and the number of those attending during the 19 days of each Bahá'í month.

In Mongolia, many families live in 'gers' – traditional tents in which more than half the people of Mongolia live, both in the countryside and in the ever-increasing ger districts around the cities. A ger is on average four metres in diameter and usually has between four and ten occupants. Wooden or wattle and daub houses on the outskirts of Ulaanbaatar or other towns may be a little larger (or even smaller) but do not always have more free space. Those Mongolian Bahá'ís who live in apartments share with many extended family members or even with the landlord's family. These family or housemate members are not always Bahá'ís, making it difficult to hold regular formal meetings in one's home. Therefore, formal devotional gatherings are held in the few larger apartments, roomy gers or public centres where more friends can gather. Informal devotional gatherings occur more frequently as individuals visit their friends and family members and find an opportunity to say prayers

with them. Bahá'ís are encouraged to share with their
family and friends the word of God and the Bahá'í
prayers in this informal way. Those individuals who offer
such impromptu devotional events to their friends usually
find them rewarding and that their acquaintances
respond very positively.

Except on specially organized formal occasions, the
programme for prayer meetings is usually not set in
advance. All the individuals gathered will have either
their own prayer books or be provided with one by their
host or a friend and will read a prayer or a passage from
the scriptures. Many people know a number of prayers
by heart. Even if there are specially chosen readers for a
set programme, after they have read others who wish to
say a prayer often say their own. There is no accepted
order for reading such as clockwise or anticlockwise or
children first then adults, etc. Each one feels the right
time and finds an opportunity for himself or herself to
read a prayer. Usually a large number of the friends
attending say a prayer each and sometimes more than
one. Children are very keen participants and say prayers
that they know by heart with confidence. The spontane-
ity of devotionals and the high percentage of participants
creates a very spiritual and united atmosphere.

The most well-used prayer book is a translation of the
Malaysian white prayer book but there are also smaller
prayer books. In Mongolia, a number of prayers and quotations from the writings of Bahá'u'lláh have been set to
beautiful music and many friends throughout Mongolia
will sing one or more of these during devotional gatherings. When one friend begins, all those who know the
prayer in question will join in melodiously and serenely
and the effect is very moving. A few of the Bahá'ís chant

the prayers in the Mongolian traditional style. A particularly skilled older gentleman from the South Gobi, who is a long-standing member of the National Spiritual Assembly of Mongolia, often chants his prayers or the holy word of God in the traditional mode, with a joyous and serene smile. His style is particularly melodious and touching. Those friends who know prayers in Russian, English or Arabic often read or sing these as well.

Nineteen Day Feast in Ulaanbaatar
Semira Manaseki

I was pregnant with Daryon, my second boy, when after eight years I came back to visit Mongolia in September 2000. This visit, unlike my previous one, was for work and I was due to spend ten very busy days piloting a medical research project which could bring me back to live in Mongolia.

I was drained with a flu caught on the long plane ride from Geneva to Ulaanbaatar and only with some effort managed to attend a Feast that had been scheduled at the Ulaanbaatar local Bahá'í Centre. I arrived only a few moments before the programme was due to start. Although returning to Mongolia and visiting the Bahá'í community was in itself rather emotional for me, what moved me tremendously was the devotional programme. A couple of familiar people, and some unfamiliar ones, stood gently and in reverence around a beautifully decorated low table at one end of the room. The table was decorated with a picture of 'Abdu'l-Bahá on a porcelain plate, some flowers and a few small candles. After silence was established, those standing began singing in a most melodious tone the prayer of Bahá'u'lláh revealed in the

Síyáh-Chál: 'God is sufficient unto me; He verily is the All-sufficing! In Him let the trusting trust.'[6] They sang this in harmony in Mongolian, English and Russian. Another prayer in Mongolian was sung, then two passages from the writings were read and another prayer in Mongolian sung. The whole experience filled me with a joy I could not contain. The programme continued as individuals sitting around the room on chairs and on the floor spontaneously read prayers or sang other prayers set to inspiring melodies. Others joined in the chanting and created a deeply spiritual atmosphere. The programme only came to an end when there was a long silence during which no one else made a contribution.

It was a comforting feeling to find myself so unfamiliar with the Bahá'í community I had left eight years before. It proved yet again the dynamic and organic process involved in the spread of the Cause of God that exerts such transforming power upon lives so apparently remote from its source.

Malaysian Devotionals

Bahá'ís everywhere are striving to increase the number of study circles, children's classes and devotional meetings. The International Teaching Centre has pointed out that while devotional meetings 'often begin with encouraging believers inspired by their institute course on spiritual life to undertake such meetings on their own', 'another approach that has resulted in an expansion in number previously not contemplated has been to hold devotional gatherings in the homes of non-Bahá'ís, who sometimes organize the meetings themselves'.[7]

Employing this arrangement over a six-month period, the believers in Malaysia were able to increase tenfold the devotional meetings in their advanced clusters and the level of participation by 40 per cent.[8]

Here are some examples of devotional meetings in Malaysia.

Devotional Meetings with a Theme
Doraisamy Suppiah

The Bahá'í community of Cuepacs in the vicinity of Kuala Lumpur, Malaysia, organizes thematic devotional meetings as a means of attracting friends of the Faith. Members of the community serve as teachers to a regular service project which offers neighbourhood education for children and junior youth from which nearly 70 children have benefited. These youth, children and parents have been attending many devotional gatherings.

When the public school examinations are near, the community organizes a devotional meeting to offer prayers for the education of children. Neighbours and friends who are already familiar with the community attend the session.

Prayers and writings on the theme of education of children are selected. The programme combines group chanting, prayers and music played from a CD. Individuals with good voices are asked to read or chant several of the prayers and writings.

Another theme has been a devotional meeting for departed souls. The friends are requested to bring along to this devotional meeting a photograph of the departed family member. All the photos are placed befittingly on a table with candles and flowers to create a dignified and spiritual setting. A selection of prayers and writings on the progress of the soul in the world of God are included in the programme. The environment of the centre or home in which the devotional is held is appropriately arranged to provide a prayerful atmosphere.

Campaign for Devotional Meetings in Cluster N4
Doraisamy Suppiah

N4 in one of the priority clusters in the north of Peninsular Malaysia and has become of hub of institute activities. To give the devotional meetings a big boost, the Local Spiritual Assembly of Sungai Petani selected the month of April 2003 for a campaign. The coordinator for devotional meetings visited every family and gave them encouragement to open their homes for weekly devotional meetings. This effort resulted in 39 devotional meetings. With continued encouragement, many of the families are now giving more attention to this activity. A few families spend an entire day preparing the devotional meeting in the evening. They make refreshments, buy flowers to decorate their home, invite fellow Bahá'ís to help with the arrangements and pray for the seekers to come. One of the friends decided to dedicate the whole day to inviting non-Bahá'ís, family members and friends to the devotional meeting held in his home in the evening. He even goes out of his way to invite to the devotional meeting people he has just met that day.

Devotional Meetings Change Community Life
Doraisamy Suppiah

The Segamat community in southern Malaysia has seen a great revival of Bahá'í community life resulting from the initiative of two families who have focused on devotional meetings.

The devotional meetings, which are held every Sunday, originally had only a brief programme but they have now grown to being an hour long. There is group chanting, reading from the writings, recital and chanting of prayers by individuals and several prayers and music played from a CD. The friends all sit in a circle. The arrangement and order of the programme is so well designed that the friends are surprised that even children are able to sit through this one hour programme.

The families and friends decided on potluck arrangements for refreshments and the food is usually abundant. The group has now grown to 40 participants. The families have managed to bring together many friends who had not been coming to Bahá'í activities and there are also a number of seekers who attend regularly.

Bhakti Vandana in India
Dr A. K. Merchant

Our usual devotional meetings are held in the homes of several Bahá'ís according to a rota set out on a Calendar of Events provided at the Nineteen Day Feasts. Believers are welcome to take their friends to any of these homes provided they first inform the host family.

But for the past four months as part of our Institute Campaign, a special devotional meeting described as Bhakti Vandana is being held at the National Bahá'í Centre every Saturday. This has a structured programme. A group of Bahá'ís and sometimes even non-Bahá'í friends team up to prepare in advance a selection of prayers and readings from the Bahá'í and other holy texts. These are chanted or sung accompanied by Indian musical instruments such as the harmonium, the tabla, the guitar and the keyboard. Occasionally these weekly programmes may be given a theme, for example, 'Unity in Diversity', 'Religions for Communal Harmony', 'We are the World' and so on. Friends who participate in these performances are youth from the community, volunteers serving at the House of Worship, Bahá'í and non-Bahá'í children who attend the weekly children's classes and members of the Bahá'í Temple choir. Each group is given the responsibility for a particular weekend.

Most of those who sing are amateurs, although a few are as good as professional singers. Invitation cards giving the dates of two upcoming Saturday programmes are distributed in the neighbourhood and at the Temple among interested visitors. In addition, some individual Bahá'ís distribute the invitations among friends in their own locality.

The audience comprises both Bahá'í and non-Bahá'í individuals, children and families. The average number of participants is 80. At the end of the programme we announce that those who would like to join the study circle or send their children to our children's moral education classes are welcome to do so and the names of the contact persons are given. These activities also take place in the National Bahá'í Centre.

Finally, everyone is invited to partake of refreshments, including tea and coffee, which is served outside on the lawns of the Bahá'í Centre. During this time Bahá'ís interact with their guests, who often ask about the Faith; a few also request introductory literature.

Experience has shown that these weekly devotional meetings are popular and that people enjoy attending them.

Devotional Meetings in Panchgani, India
Mahnaz Afshin

The Bahá'í Academy in Panchgani, India, was established in 1982 as a centre dedicated to the advanced study of the Bahá'í Faith and its teachings and to the training of teachers, pioneers, administrators and scholars. It offers short- and long-term courses in a number of subject areas and also assists Bahá'ís in the Commonwealth of Independent States of the former Soviet Union by conducting workshops for institute directors and teachers.

> Devotional meetings are conducted regularly every Tuesday at 11 a.m. at the Bahá'í Academy. All the staff from the director to the workers attend this programme. It begins with slow music followed by prayers which are chanted or recited by everyone in his or her own language. Interestingly, most of the people who attend are not Bahá'ís. If there is a guest present, he or she is invited to say a few words of inspiration.

Other devotional meetings are held in the homes of local Bahá'ís:

> Ten days before every devotional meeting the friends inform and invite guests to attend. They do this at least three times to ensure a good number of participants. The result of such efforts by one Bahá'í friend was the attendance of 15 non-Bahá'ís.
>
> The meeting starts with Indian classical music, for example a recording of Ravi Shankar on the sitar. After that, each person reads a passage from his own religious literature or from the Bahá'í writings selected for the

occasion. This adds to the unity of thought. Sometimes devotional songs are sung by all the participants. The programme ends with a prayer for unity.

Afterwards refreshments are served. The host or other Bahá'ís gathered answer any questions the guests may have.

The host makes sure that all leave the house with a feeling of joy and happiness and enhanced love towards each other.

Devotional meetings are also held in the villages nearby.

In one village, usually between 10 and 20 people from three families attend a simple devotional programme. Every Saturday night, at around 8:30, they gather to read Bahá'í prayers, selections from the Hidden Words and passages from the Hindu scriptures.

Australian Experiences

Devotions under Some of the Southern Sky
Dicy Hall

In Australia, many have the perception that interest in religion is weak and that developing a devotional attitude is not popular. BE 159 will be remembered for the strengthening of systematic individual and group initiatives in children's education, the study circle process and creative devotional meetings – and for being the year that many Australians proved that there is no foundation for this assumption.

The striving of the friends towards service in these key areas has met with every success. But success is not always easy to predict. It is wonderful to open up the doors of the Bahá'í community and invite people to these events. In some cases people attend and find more than they ever hoped for – these people may become Bahá'ís as a result of their experience. Other successes seem to come to the Bahá'ís themselves, however: a deeper appreciation of their own faith, sincerity in their friendships and a love for the divine materials they utilize and study. These effects are perhaps more significant than the Bahá'ís anticipated. In the course of giving to others, these friends are being 'renewed'.

In Australia, setting up devotional meetings may appear at first to be daunting. There must be a link between the design of the programme content, the atmosphere and the target audience.

Otherwise, how can one create a relationship between people so that they will attend again and again? How does one meet the challenge of devising a programme that will illuminate the attributes by which we live – love, peace, beauty, honour, respect and so on? The devotional meetings described below answer these questions. They have been successful, simple and meaningful.

YOUTH DEVOTIONALS

Our family, which lives in Sydney, intends to hold a monthly devotional meeting for youth – partly because our children are at that age and partly because it has become disturbing to them to care so much for their friends and not have a tangible way to show it. The youth in our family have certainly 'taught' their friends and gone to Bahá'í meetings with some of them. Some of their friends have attended Bahá'í classes at the high school periodically and are quite comfortable with the bit of knowledge they have.

After consultation with our children and Bahá'í friends we are planning a meeting open to youth who are firm in their own religion, to those who have never been asked what they believe and to those who are actually intrigued with the Bahá'í Faith or are Bahá'ís. Experience indicates the best time to hold these will be on a Sunday afternoon. The programme will either begin with a lunch barbecue followed by a devotional time or vice-versa. We intend to invite a dozen youth of diverse backgrounds. One idea we have is to use music to develop a bond and then read twice a quotation that provides a provocative question about moral development. Supporting material – prayers and readings from the faith traditions – will be placed on the central table. Time will be given to the youth to ponder each reading. Then each person who cares to share his or her account or understanding of this moral experience will speak. The youth might like to read more from the displayed materials or play more music. The programme will end when the participants wish. Getting it right probably worries us more than the youth, who will have a good time regardless!

SERENE HEARTS

Our local community's Teaching Committee has recently held the popular Tranquillity Zone model. Called 'Serene Hearts', its logo is on all invitations and is now recognizable to community members. This gives it an identity which has become part of the vision and this is perhaps important to consider. This model uses readings chosen mostly from the House of Worship programmes. (Sydney is lucky enough to have a House of Worship and the programmes are carefully compiled according to a theme.) Readings used are 'multifaith' prayers and the readers are selected and rehearsed before the event. The average number of readers are three to four. The formal part of the programme is readings in English but then all who wish to pray, in whatever language, are invited to do so. The atmosphere of tranquillity is achieved with the central candles and flowers. Soft music is played in the background, using classical or nature tapes. Between the readings or prayers the music is lifted.

Invitations are given to Bahá'ís who have friends who would like to attend. Posters in local shopping centres and specific shops that showcase 'nature' are used to attract the public. The meetings are held once a month on a Sunday afternoon at 3 p.m. in a local library meeting room and run for 45 to 60 minutes. The public attend but the majority who come are Bahá'ís. Children attend and they often pray.

The committee is reviewing Serene Hearts. The first series of meetings was successful but the exposure to the public needs adjustment as it is the least successful part of the effort. Attendance would be higher if more advertising were used. The reality is that with the House of Worship nearby and having a service there on the same day complete with choir and a glorious atmosphere, many people choose to go there instead. For the people who do come to Serene Hearts, bonds of friendship have been formed.

TRANQUILLITY ZONE

Another very similar model is used elsewhere in our cluster and is called 'Tranquillity Zone'. The group that organizes this advertises in the diary section of the local paper. As a result of this and the personal invitations issued at their local stalls, there is a very good turnout of at least nine guests plus the Bahá'ís. Because the event is held in the local library, people also come in off the street.

The readings are from all faith traditions and in between each reading the music is soothing. Most of the readers are Bahá'ís but on occasion guests read. The atmosphere of the room is the beautiful 'candle, cushion and cosy' style.

Although these meetings are held once a month, reviewing them indicates the need to have readers practice what they will read – partially because it is hard to see by the light of candles! The popularity of this group's efforts is growing and people have commented that it is a beautiful and relaxing time.

PERSONAL DEVOTIONAL MEETINGS

Already nearing the end of its first year, a series of personal devotional meetings organized by four close friends (two married couples) and their children has a special family atmosphere. They realized they had friends to whom they wanted to introduce the Faith – or the spiritual atmosphere of the Faith – and although initially they were unsure how to proceed, the turn of world events presented them with an opportunity.

They decided to say prayers for the state of world affairs. For the first meeting, they began the evening with a dinner (although now they begin with the devotions) and then had prayers. Everyone they asked to attend the first meeting accepted the invitation. They then decided to make the next dinner a potluck to give everyone a feeling of involvement in the evening. This sense of ownership of the occasion extends to a friendly push from the guests to hold meetings regularly – which is a true sign of the importance of these warm, embracing devotions.

The prayers and readings come from diverse sources. The friends live quite close to the House of Worship in Sydney so they are aware of the need to have a broadly based programme but even this they have extended to include the preferences of guests, including native North American traditions. The programme lasts for 20 minutes and everyone has a chance to read. They make use of candles and they play guitar but they keep it simple.

When the bombing occurred in Bali, which greatly affected Australia, a meeting was arranged at short notice. This attracted new people who would otherwise not have been aware of the Bahá'í Faith but who came to the meeting to reflect on this event.

These friends are experiencing a special bond and the love and hospitality is continually a reward in itself. For all of us who wonder what success is, perhaps this is one sort of reward we can give ourselves.

DEVOTIONAL MEETINGS FOR HEALING

Outside of the cluster and up in the beautiful mountains nearby is a very special situation that has created the need for devotional meetings. One of the dearly loved Bahá'í friends has become critically ill and his family offer meetings of urgent prayer to Bahá'u'lláh which reach out in comfort to all the friends, who are deeply distressed. The meetings focus on words that provide a sense of, and a prayer for, healing. From all the sacred writings, each person who attends reads whatever he or she has chosen to read. Beautiful music – classical or Bahá'í prayers and songs – is played as background. Two of these meetings have been held in the family's home and one in the hospital. Large groups of people gathered for the home meetings: some were specially invited guests and some were community and other Bahá'í guests. Food and refreshment were provided in abundance after these meetings.

The meeting held in the hospital created a healing haven for the staff and other patients who were drawn into the circle. It was held in a beautiful 'reflection room' within the hospital which previously had been kept locked and was unused. Some 15 nurses, hospital workers and other patients gathered there in prayer with the family and guests. The motive for this prayer meeting was that 'everybody needs prayer, so why don't we use this room?'

After that meeting one patient remarked, 'No one else ever did this for me' and was moved that he had been welcomed and included. A beautiful photograph of the Shrine of the Báb and the Terraces as well as music inspired one nurse to visit the House of Worship. She then told a friend who also visited and now wants to learn more about the Faith.

'REFRESH AND GLADDEN MY SPIRIT'

This same community holds a monthly 'Refresh and Gladden My Spirit' devotional meeting in a school hall in the mountains. They use a booklet of prayers of all faiths for their readings, which makes things easy, and they advertise in the local paper. People who come once continue to come and there are many who go on to participate in other Bahá'í activities, including the core activities. As evidence of their success, these meetings are now multi-plying. From this original meeting the community has gone on to create four new meetings which are held in dif-ferent parts of the neighbouring mountain sectors.

Tranquillity Zone in Alice Springs
Ladan Wise

We advertise our devotional meetings in Alice Springs as 'Tranquillity Zones' but during the recent war in Iraq we called them 'prayers for peace'. We used to hold them every fortnight on Tuesdays but now they are held each week. Bahá'ís invite their friends and work associates, we put up posters at a local 'hippy' cafe and the library and we also place ads in the local paper each week.

We hold the devotionals at a Bahá'í home that has a kind of 'hall' attached to it that was once used as a yoga centre, so the residents of our town seem to be familiar with it being used for that purpose. Between three and 20 people attend each time. Although on average 20 per cent of those who participate are not Bahá'ís, we have found that they rarely attend more than once and we are assess-ing why this might be. Children come only occasionally.

The programme consists of 15 to 20 short passages from all the holy writings on specific themes such as race unity, love and justice. There is usually about 75 per cent Bahá'í content. We sometimes include prayers or short inspirational stories on the topic. Normally, three people are chosen from among those who have attended to read the passages in turn.

Music is used throughout. I have made a compilation of ambient music – not necessarily 'Bahá'í' music and usually with no words – that I play in the background and turn up louder in between each reading for a minute or so, which provides time for reflection. Sometimes this is replaced by live guitar music and a passage from the Bahá'í holy writings which is sung part the way through the programme or at the end.

Those who attend the devotional meetings are made aware of the firesides/discussion evening at the same venue the next night. So far we have not connected them to children's classes or training institute programmes but we are looking into this, as this may be one reason why some people do not return.

The Tranquillity Zones are non-threatening gatherings and we do not find it too difficult to invite our non-Bahá'í friends to them. In general, we have found them to be successful, with some seekers attending regularly. The meetings have enabled seekers to pray with members of the Bahá'í community and to develop bonds of friendship and some have subsequently become Bahá'ís.

* * *

Many creative and heartfelt attempts to provide a devotional environment in our little part of Australia are being made. These personal and community meetings are taking on forms that go far beyond sitting around a table saying prayers by 'ourselves'. Opening up the doors under these southern skies is not as difficult, and people are not as unresponsive, as we may have previously thought!

European Experiences

Classical Music in Switzerland
Mahchid Fatio

Many devotional gatherings centre on music, as we recognize that 'We, verily, have made music as a ladder for your souls, a means whereby they may be lifted up unto the realm on high'.[9] Using personal invitations, telephone and email, a Bahá'í in a small town in Switzerland invites both non-Bahá'ís and local Bahá'ís to devotional meetings in her home on the third Tuesday of every month from 8:00 p.m. to 9:00 p.m.

On the evening of the devotional meeting, I put fresh flowers and candles in the room where the devotionals are held. I select readings mainly from the writings and prayers of Bahá'u'lláh but also from those of 'Abdu'l-Bahá and the Báb. Often, non-Bahá'ís read the selections. Classical music is played for a few minutes at the beginning, in the middle and at the end of each devotional meeting.

From the beginning, the devotional meetings have been attended by a number of people: between two and six non-Bahá'ís and two to five Bahá'ís. Everyone has expressed how much they appreciate the readings, and far from finding the session too long, they say they wish there were more readings. After the devotionals soft drinks are served.

So successful have these devotional meetings been that I now hold them throughout the year, even during the holiday period.

Devotional Meetings in the Netherlands
Joanna M. Tahzib-Thomas

When the House of Justice first called for these devotional meetings there was a natural initial reservation among some of the Bahá'ís as to whether people would be interested enough to attend a prayer meeting. Then 9/11 happened and the candlelit prayer meetings that took place spontaneously throughout the whole world brought the realization that the House of Justice does not ask us to do something without a reason.

Gradually some 'prayer meetings' (in the Dutch language there is no word for 'devotional') began to be held with only Bahá'ís attending. Some communities had already been holding prayer meetings for the Bahá'ís on Sunday mornings. Things did not really go forward as they should till the Memorandum on devotional meetings came from the World Centre (see appendix 1). Slowly the concept began to be more well understood. Several communities/clusters changed the name from 'prayer meetings' to 'inspirational' or 'meditative meetings', which were more attractive to a wider range of people.

But the communities that held the meetings still had to open their doors to everyone. It needed courage and reaching out. In some communities collaboration with interreligious organizations and involvement in interfaith dialogue provided an opening to invite people to the devotionals. Gradually, through the encouragement of the National Assembly and the assistants in each cluster, this concept began to develop and grow. Soon friends and neighbours were being invited. We were getting the idea.

In addition, because holding devotional meetings was to be the result of Ruhi book 1 study circles, this further stimulated the process and things began moving. Several communities combined devotional meetings with children's classes very successfully, with lunch added at the end. Descriptions of some of the most successful devotional meetings are included below.

We still have a way to go before we invite more and more non-Bahá'ís but we are getting there. As word gets around of how much non-Bahá'ís are drawn to the spiritual, peaceful atmosphere of the meetings, more and more are springing up. The Netherlands has a high percentage of non-churchgoers and people miss the devotional atmosphere and community life. If our communities become more attractive, surely more and more souls thirsty for spirituality and meditation will come.

Meditative Meetings in Nijmegen
Dr Charles Hamburger

When we decided to host devotional meetings, we gave a lot of thought to finding a form that would be attractive and would not mar the consecrated character of the meeting. We avoided the term 'prayer meetings' in the announcements and chose 'meditative meetings' instead. In Nijmegen such meetings are organized regularly by other religious groups, for example by the Buddhists, and in other spiritual centres. We wished to distinguish ourselves with regard to the form and content of our meetings and finally decided on a programme one and a half hours long with different parts.

We decide beforehand on the theme for a cycle of four meetings, for example 'The Soul' or 'The New Day'. For each meeting we carefully select a small number of texts from the Bahá'í writings and from other holy books.

We always begin with live music, usually by an amateur ensemble, for example, a flute or small choir. We choose the music to suit the theme. We always recite the texts two times after each other with a long pause in between. This meditative part we close with music.

After a break when coffee and tea are served, we try to stimulate an exchange of thoughts with several questions based on the text. We split up into small groups of three to four persons with a Bahá'í as facilitator.

If the time allows we end the meeting with a creative activity, for example, mandala drawings. This we do very peacefully. There is no talking during this time.

Prayer Meetings with Study Circles
Amelia Taeed

Two clusters (Deventer/Diepenveen and Apeldoorn) hold joint devotional meetings once a month. In Dutch the meetings are called 'Prayer Meetings'. The meetings are in two parts. The first part is the devotional itself. The prayers and readings are chosen mostly from the Bahá'í writings but sometimes are taken from other sacred writings or even from the works of philosophers. Some participants chant a Bahá'í prayer. Everyone participates actively in this programme, even the non-Bahá'ís. It goes around in a circle. We finish this part with the prayer 'Remover of Difficulties'. The prayers are always said in four or more different languages including Persian or Arabic chanting – everyone appreciates that. We start and end with music, usually classical Western music or Bahá'í-inspired music from a CD.

The second part is a spiritual training from the book *Reflections on the Life of the Spirit*.

One person, who has followed the tutor training, takes the role of the tutor.

Most of the people who come are friends of the Bahá'ís or become friends through firesides and some are non-Bahá'í partners. Recently some Iranian asylum seekers who are interested in the Faith have been participating. Further, we have an Iraqi friend, and a Polish neighbour who comes every three months to the Netherlands. Also a person from the Caribbean has recently become a Bahá'í. People come from different places and towns. This devotional meeting has taken place in Apeldoorn for more than 25 years, although it has changed from its original form.

For a long time, this gathering was held in one cluster one month and in the other cluster the next. However, one of the friends requested to have the meetings at her home all the time so that her non-Bahá'í husband would be able to participate.

Several children and youth from four to 21 years old participate in the first part of the programme and then they go to another room to have their children and youth classes. During consultation, the youth indicated that they would like to have a Ruhi study circle during the children's classes so they can take their non-Bahá'í friends as well, so we are considering adding this.

The atmosphere of spirituality is felt very much and the prayer meetings are usually attended by more Bahá'ís than is the case with the other gatherings! We think it is a successful activity, since there has been no break all these years and so many people attend.

Devotional Meetings with Children's Classes
Dini Hilbron

During the second year of the Five Year Plan it seemed impossible to maintain the only existing Local Spiritual Assembly in one of the clusters. When five of the friends moved away from Culemborg, leaving fewer than nine adult Bahá'ís in this small city in the middle of the Netherlands, the effect was dramatic. It took a lot of energy of the friends in the cluster to keep the activities going and to think long term, now that there was no longer an Assembly to provide a supportive structure.

During a consultation with the Auxiliary Board member for Protection and her assistant at the beginning of 2002, the friends reflected on the emotional and practical effects brought on by the loss of the only Assembly in their cluster and then moved on to consider how to get busy constructively with the new possibilities that the cluster formation and the Five Year Plan had to offer.

In the middle of 2002 the assistants to both the Propagation and Protection boards together with a Bahá'í from Culemborg organized the first meeting for all the friends in the cluster. During this meeting, a forerunner of the reflection meetings, a lot of attention was given to the meanings enshrined in the House of Justice letters about the Five Year Plan. Through this the friends present realized cluster formation is an instrument of growth, that we can encourage each other in our clusters and that individual initiative and collective plans can take place and flourish. In addition, a working group was formed to organize the Nineteen Day Feasts and the holy days.

In the autumn of 2002 the first reflection meeting took place in this cluster and the friends were confronted with the fact that the only core activity in the cluster was the study circle started two years previously with a nucleus of motivated friends. All kinds of suggestions were given of how to breathe new life into the previous meditative meetings and organize training in Ruhi book 3 as soon as possible so that a children's class could be started. Also, the study circle tutor organized an extra meeting based on the Australian document about organizing devotional meetings.

Several participants of the existing study circle were so inspired that they decided to get busy working on the results of this consultation and as a result came to a creative solution that suited this cluster and the various Bahá'í families with young children.

Since the end of 2002 a working group has been organizing a devotional meeting for adults, young adults and youth – for Bahá'ís and others – once a month on a Sunday morning. This meeting is from 10:30 till 12:00 and is held in the home of a Bahá'í family. At the same time a children's class is held in the next door neighbour's home, also a Bahá'í family. This children's class is attended by ten to twelve children from one to ten years of age. The children's class begins at 10:30. The parents then go to the neighbour's home where the devotional meeting has been arranged. At 12:00 all the children go next door where the host and hostess of the devotional meeting and the others present have prepared a lunch. Everyone eats together, young and old, Bahá'í and non-Bahá'í. This creative formula has been working the last few months to everyone's satisfaction and has a great capacity to grow and develop.

During the devotional meeting texts from the writings are read interchangeably with music. Everyone is encouraged to bring suitable music and texts from other holy books. Before the meeting the choice is consulted on with the hostess, who chooses the music. During the first half hour coffee and tea are served for everyone and news exchanged, especially about the children. At 11:00 the devotional meeting begins with music followed by prayer. Then everyone reads a text or prayer as he or she feels moved to do so. This 'freedom within a clear structure' seems to give everyone the most effective meditative possibilities. At 12:00 the children come in, full of stories and usually with something they have made themselves. It is heartwarming to see that the children, young and older, have got to know each other so well and enjoy being together and helping each other.

All the friends in the cluster are happy with this approach. Rather than waiting until all the circumstances are optimally present, a beginning has been made based on the conviction that this combined teaching activity will continue to grow!

A Hum and a Drum
Gary Villiers-Stuart

The Burnlaw Centre is tucked away on the hillside of a remote Northumberland valley. Over the last 20 years a deserted farmhouse, cottage and crumbling farm buildings have been transformed into a thriving community of five private dwellings, a 45 acre organic small holding and an education centre. The centre is inspired and informed by Bahá'í, Buddhist and environmental thinking and is run by some of the residents of Burnlaw. It describes itself as a place for 'Learning Creativity and the Soul'. Its educational programme caters for all ages – youngsters, teenagers, young adults, older souls – and those of a mystical persuasion. Nature, dance, music, percussion, holy text, world wisdom and consultation are used as educational tools and contexts to enable soul insight.

The centre encourages and uses many forms of prayer and mediation. During our weekly community unity feasts we use the prayer of spoken devotions and prayer in the form of music from both Bahá'í and many other wisdom traditions of the world. There is music in prayer and prayer in music. Then there is the prayer of silent reflective listening. This takes place daily and also in community unity feasts. There is also the prayer of dynamic meditation; silent and conscious walking is often incorporated into weekends of reflective study. There is the prayer of community service: often weekend and week-long events incorporate some sort of cooperative work to achieve some public good. Then there is the prayer of the study of the holy texts, when hearts are encouraged to ascend and open their souls to the realm of inner significances. All these and more can be used as ways to commune with the Loved One.

Prayer is to do with nearness. Prayer becomes potent when the soul is enkindled, when one relaxes into an inward smile, when one feels a sense of wonderment, optimism and gratefulness. During this process one's inward world receives an insight, an inspiration, a solution to a problem.

The best collective prayer generates the sweetest of atmospheres. The silence is alive with a subtle but perceptible energy. The self no longer feels so self-conscious. The aftermath atmosphere is permeated with an extraordinary richness of exhilaration.

We mark one festival with what is known locally as 'a hum and a drum'. There are perhaps 30 people in the room, each with some sort of percussive instrument. A slow pulse rhythm begins. As the rhythm develops, counter rhythms come into play and soon the room is alive with a network of different rhythms, all making a diverse but harmonious whole. As the rhythm develops so too does a melody of improvised song. The group forms a greater identity which seems to control the way the voice and percussion organically rise and fall. As time passes the intensity swells into a great loudness. After this there is space for the presence of the quiet and the harmonious. Someone starts a long low hum. Others join, giving the sound a richness of harmony, tone and overtone. Someone else is inspired to sing a line from the Tablet of Aḥmad; others start improvising on that line; it becomes a mantra; others sing other lines from the holy writings; there is now a medley of humming, holy writing and song. The atmosphere becomes pregnant with an invigorating beauty, a sense of oneness, a sense of wellbeing. There is a listening, a fragrance, a beauty of sound, sentiment and an improvised creativity. We have become enraptured by His smile, His good pleasure. We are literally spellbound. It is a timeless moment, a moment of beautiful intensity. Eventually the energy of that listening attentiveness comes to an end. The sounds fade into an intense silence. The silence is held for a short time, and then begin chattering and laughter, hugs and smiles as the group moves into a different atmosphere but still the atmosphere of the paradise of His good pleasure.

I know we have all experienced what I would describe as a 'Lote Tree' moment. It is as though we have reached a richness of atmosphere beyond which there is nowhere further to go. My intuition tells me that the scattering angels are scattering and the whole of creation has been infinitesimally enriched. I know that what we have experienced is pure grace, the richest possible food for the soul.

Pacific Experiences

Candlelight Devotions in Tonga
Soheyla and Sohrab Bolouri and Don Blanks

The Polynesian Kingdom of Tonga, also known as the Friendly Islands, lies in the South Pacific on the international date line and is made up of hundreds of small islands in four island groups. Tonga is one of the world's few remaining constitutional monarchies and is the only South Pacific country never to have been colonized by a foreign power. It is ruled by His Majesty King Taufa'ahau Tupou IV. The people are deeply religious, mainly Christian, and are ardent churchgoers. The Bahá'í Faith was established in Tonga in 1954, during the Ten Year Crusade, and has grown rapidly in recent years.

Basically we have two types of devotional meetings. The first is organized by Local Spiritual Assemblies. The programme usually consists of a few prayers, reading from the Bahá'í holy writings and a couple of songs or music. This method has been quite successful in some areas but not so successful in others. In general, however, so far very few have attracted any participants other than Bahá'ís.

The second type of devotional meeting is organized by individuals and these seem to have more success. The programmes vary according to the taste of the host and the people they wish to attract. For example, one youth chooses different themes such as love, worship, spirit and so on for each devotional meeting and prepares quotations on the selected subject from different holy books. The meetings are held at night with candle lights in the room and soft music in the background. The programme starts with a Bahá'í prayer followed by the writings and closes with prayer. This method attracts many non-Bahá'í youth. Another individual includes many readings from the Bible and even some Christian hymn-singing and this has attracted quite a few people.

At present we have tons of study circles, increasing numbers of children's classes being run in neighbourhoods and one devotional meeting per village.

Walking in Tahiti
Daniel Pierce

Tahiti is in French Polynesia in the Society Island group. Most of the people are Christian but the Bahá'í Faith arrived in 1920 when John and Louise Bosch stayed on the Pacific island for five months.

Tahiti is not very representative of the Pacific Bahá'í communities and should perhaps be seen as a case apart. Nevertheless, it seems that our efforts to share the word of God with our friends are having similar effects as elsewhere in the world.

Recently, in response to the Five Year Plan, three Bahá'ís spent a week travel teaching on Moorea. They walked around the island sharing the Bahá'í message with anyone interested and offering to say prayers with families. Several families accepted and were very happy to receive the visitors. Most had not heard of the Faith and some knew of it only vaguely but all were attracted by the approach of the teachers and appreciated the prayers.

At the prayer meetings the three Bahá'ís said prayers in different languages and on various themes and the hosts sometimes joined in by reading the Bahá'í prayers themselves. The families were very touched when the Bahá'í teachers left the small booklet 'Words of God' with them.

On returning, the teaching team visited two families in Papeete with ties to Vanuatu who had already invited them to come and say prayers. The first session was a success with all the family members present, some using the Bahá'í prayers. The families have now asked for Bahá'í activity or education for their children.

In Papeete, two families hold regular prayer meetings in their homes, attended mostly by children in the neighbourhood with some adults taking part. The devotionals are very simple, consisting of reading prayers and singing Bahá'í scripture.

The community of Paea holds a successful devotional meeting every Wednesday night. Between four and ten people usually attend. One seeker attends regularly and as a result has agreed to attend a Ruhi book 1 study circle. She thoroughly enjoys this, especially the learning environment and the spirit of unity and sharing. She is very attracted by the Bahá'í scripture and prayers and loves the devotional meeting where she 'recharges her batteries'. This devotional meeting is usually opened with some words of welcome which are followed by songs and choral pieces (Bahá'í prayers and passages from the scriptures). After this are one or several rounds of prayers in French, Tahitian and English and reading of the scripture. Now and again there are some meditative choral pieces.

After the meeting people sit and chat over a cup of tea and often this continues late into the night.

Sunday Devotions in the Marshall Islands
Robin Bell

Rairok is one of the largest Bahá'í communities of the Marshall Islands. It is situated on Majuro atoll, the capital of this scattered island nation in the midst of the Pacific Ocean.

Each Sunday morning the Bahá'ís of Rairok meet for Sunday devotions. This gathering, a focal point for the community for many years, is held in a separate building of a friend's home. Prior to this room's role as a base for the local community it had been used as a dressmaking centre and is commonly known as 'The Sewing House'.

Before each Sunday gathering, the children, including many from families who are not yet Bahá'ís, congregate for their children's classes. At the last count over 40 children were in attendance. Some stay on afterwards, whilst others prefer to play outside by the ocean.

At 11:00, the official start time, one or two of the friends arrive and warmly greet each other. By about 11:30 the room is full and after some stories of the week's events (most of which are highly amusing), the friends settle and listen to the host collectively greet everyone – giving special welcomes to friends from other Marshall Islands communities, to international guests and to those unfamiliar faces, perhaps seekers, invited and attending the gathering. Prayers and holy verses begin to be recited, often at first by the children.

Both the English and Marshallese languages are used and, as the Rairok community is particularly rich in its

Pacific diversity, prayers are often also recited in the languages of Kiribati, Fiji, Tuvalu and Tonga.

Without a fixed plan, friends offer their prayers as and when they feel ready to do so. Some offer quotations from their Ruhi books used for study circles, whilst others read from their burgundy copies of *Naan ko Retino*, the Marshallese translation of the *Hidden Words*.

Spiritually nourished, the friends await the theme and facilitator of the morning's deepening. This could take the guise of a short talk regarding an upcoming holy day or be a consultation on a particular and topical aspect of the Faith, such as the role of Bahá'í parents. But in the majority of instances the facilitator will patiently divide the friends into four groups with each given a prepared copy of a particular Hidden Word in both the English and Marshallese languages.

(The *Hidden Words* are particularly important to the community at present as plans are underway to present each household in the Marshall Islands with their own Marshallese copy of these gems of divine guidance.)

The friends consult upon the meaning and message of each Hidden Word amongst themselves. After 20 minutes or so, each group recites its given verse and offers its insights to the assemblage, in both Marshallese and English, as to the theme and nature of each *Naan ko Retino*. Inevitably, each group will discover a pearl.

To end, some friends are persuaded to lead the gathering in song. Soon the Sewing House is filled with sweet island voices and natural harmonies.

The event is almost over. Perhaps time to make any announcements of events in the forthcoming days and perhaps a gentle reminder to the host and facilitator of next Sunday's meeting.

But the friends are persuaded to linger a little longer for a good cause. As it is approaching lunchtime the Rairok Bahá'í youth may offer prepared plates of local food, sandwiches and canned drinks with the proceeds directed to the needy local fund.

Tranquillity Zones

The Origin of the Tranquillity Zone
Stephen Maund

Those friends fortunate enough to have attended the Sidcot Summer School [United Kingdom] in August 1997 had the opportunity to visit the old oak-panelled library at the School, which was transformed by the use of drapes, candles, flowers and photographs of significant figures in the Faith. This 'Journey to the Heart' as it was called was the inspired work of the Dacey family, who wove music (some taped and some sung live by Conrad Lambert) and readings from the Bahá'í writings into a highly profound experience. The simple invitation to each session, which included a special one for the youth, asked attendees to prepare as if they were about to meet 'Abdu'l-Bahá.

So inspired were the friends from the Wirral who took part that they decided to hold a similar event at a fair organized by Wirral Grammar School for Girls in Bebington on 27 September 1997. Staging the event for a non-Bahá'í audience, they needed a more inclusive title. The name 'tranquillity zone' was the suggestion of David Netherwood, who was then eight years old . . .

The first 'TZ' was the most popular part of the fair and the organizers predicted in the [Bahá'í] Journal [UK]:

'This idea will be a complete success and winner of hearts wherever it is repeated.'

From *The Bahá'í Journal UK*, March–April 2002. Reprinted with the permission of the author and of the National Spiritual Assembly of the United Kingdom.

The Tranquillity Zone^{TM}
From the Tranquillity Zone Website

The Tranquillity Zone^{TM} is an initiative of the Bahá'í Community in the United Kingdom, a means of helping people attain inner peace in this crowded and frenetic world. It works by creating an atmosphere in which mind, body and spirit are soothed and made tranquil. There is no special 'spiritual technique' involved, no mantra, and no specifically religious practices.

It is organized by local communities and offered as a service to the wider public. Its primary aim is not to spread the Bahá'í Faith, although of course people's questions will be answered and they are welcome to find out more about its teachings. To prevent commercial exploitation the name 'Tranquillity Zone' has been trademarked by the National Spiritual Assembly of the Bahá'ís of the United Kingdom, the elected administrative body for the Faith in this country. For more information go to the national Website at <www.bahai.org.uk>

The Tranquillity Zone: A Basic Step-by-Step Approach

First things first:

- Who is organizing it? A group, a committee, a working party?

- Make sure you have your strategy worked out: who is the Tranquillity Zone for? where is it? when do you hold it? how far ahead of time can you gain access to set up? does everyone know their tasks? are all the tasks allocated to someone?

These are basic and obvious points but if you do not plan at the start it is amazing how easy it is to overlook something important. ('No, honestly, I thought you were bringing the keys to open up!')

- Have you thought about fire risks? Potential hazards and obstructions? Disabled access? Are you insured for this activity?

And for the event itself:

- Materials needed include the following: flowers, vases, muslin, candles and floating candles, cushions, rugs, tablecloths, rose oil and burner. These can be acquired over time, depending on the size of your venue, etc.

- Choose a room where there will be no outside distractions or noise – and make sure it's warm.

- Darken the room with dark curtains.

- Drape the muslin around the room to enhance the beauty of the space. You can even make the room look like a heavenly tent, depending on the amount of muslin you have and the shape of the room you're using!

- Arrange a low table in the middle of the room draped with a large white cloth.

- Arrange the flowers and candles around the room and on the table.

- Burn rose oil so a beautiful scent will pervade the room.

- Scatter your cushions around the floor and provide chairs for people who do not wish to sit on the floor.

SAFETY PRECAUTIONS

Anyone organizing a Tranquillity Zone is obliged to take care to ensure the safety of participants and must check that they are covered by the appropriate insurance. Candles and drapes, for instance, can come together to make a fire hazard and only fire-retardant materials should be used. There should be no candles on the floor, for safety reasons, and only floating candles or enclosed ones to be used. There must be sufficient space for participants to move safely, which means a sensible limit on numbers. Clear standard fire exit signs should also be used. These safety precautions must be taken and sound common sense used in all arrangements.

THE PROGRAMME

A warm welcome outside the Tranquillity Zone – it's important that no one sees the room beforehand. During this time it's important to tell people exactly what will happen. For example you could say:

Welcome to the Tranquillity Zone. I'm (name) and I'm a member of the local Bahá'í community.

The Tranquillity Zone is a meditative experience, a little oasis away from the hustle and bustle of life. It is a place where we can enjoy a few unhurried moments to reflect on some inspiring words with music, specially chosen to uplift the heart, rejoice the soul and refresh the spirit. A welcome escape from the pressures of life. The readings you will hear are mostly from the Bahá'í sacred writings and the music is from different traditions all over the world . . .

- One might then explain the kind of readings the people will hear and the types of music. You should also explain how long the programme will last and offer guests the opportunity to stay for refreshments afterwards.

- Always check that people have switched off their mobile phones!

- As participants go into the room rose water is sprinkled onto their hands.

- The room is darkened and lit only by 20 to 30 candles and the fragrance of roses wafts over them.

- Opening quotations are read. The prayer Blessed is the Spot has also been found appropriate at these sessions.

- Music, followed by the first set of readings on peace or happiness or whatever the first theme is, followed by a second piece of music, followed by a second set of readings, etc. until the end. There are generally about four themes and it is good to try to set out a little 'journey', e.g. Section 1: Coping with Stress; Section 2: Healing; Section 3: Hope and Love; Section 4: Life of the Soul or True Life.

- When all is finished, refreshments are served whilst music quietly plays, friendships and contact is then made.

- Guests are then invited to sign a visitor's book, take words of wisdom (a prayer, Blessed is the Spot) and take the programme of forthcoming events.

- People who leave their names and addresses are invited to all the events organized by Bahá'ís, e.g. future Tranquillity Zones, Tranquillity Feasts, firesides and other meetings.

- Experience has shown that a formal 'talk' after the Tranquillity Zone didn't work but people often stay to talk.

IDEAS FOR PROGRAMMES

- Quotations and prayers from the Bahá'í holy writings arranged around four themes (for example: peace, happiness, health and healing, friendship, spirituality, life of the soul, contentment, work).

- Writings from other scriptures or sources.

- Experience has shown that about five different quotes per theme are best, to be read slowly, clearly and maybe repeated.

- The programme lasts about 40 minutes and refreshments are served.

- Choose different pieces of music, e.g. Bahá'í choral music, classical music, meditative Celtic music, Buddhist chant, natural sounds, etc.– whatever you feel is conducive to meditation and spirituality.

FOLLOW-UP

This is easiest if the Tranquillity Zone is arranged regularly in the same place. Ensure that those attending have information about other activities that they might want to attend. But never, ever, pressure them.

The Swindon Experience

The Bahá'í community in the English town of Swindon had pioneered the use of the Tranquillity Zone in this country. A local member explained:

Our understanding of the Tranquillity Zone in Swindon is to help people take their first step along the spiritual path, on their spiritual journey. We promote the Tranquillity Zone as an oasis of calm and well-being for the body, mind and soul. It is held in a beautiful candlelit tent-like setting, surrounded by fragrant flowers and drapes. Guests can enjoy a few unhurried moments to reflect on some inspiring words mainly from the Bahá'í writings, with soothing music, specially chosen to uplift the heart and nourish the soul.

The Tranquillity Zone is a community service project which has been running for three years now. The service we are offering is that of spiritual development and spiritual enrichment. Swindon prides itself on being an economically prosperous town. But emphasis on material development only can never respond to all the needs of a human being. Prosperity in its true sense includes both material and spiritual well-being.

A SURVEY ON STRESS

We did a survey a few months ago in Swindon town centre which revealed that a great majority of people suffered stress at work and needed to find ways of dealing with it. According to the Confederation of British Industry (CBI), stress costs the UK £7 – £8 billion a year. The Health and Safety Executive (HSE) claim that around 60 per cent of consultations at GP surgeries are stress related, which can lead to depression and other illnesses.

This kind of research indicates that it's not enough to simply concentrate on economic prosperity and material well-being, because we pay the price in ill-health, sick days and low morale. We need to strike a balance by nurturing an inner strength and an awareness of our spiritual side. This can have many positive effects, including helping us handle more effectively situations which cause stress. We believe that the Tranquillity Zone is putting a bit of the spirit back into Swindon.

It is made clear that the Tranquillity Zone is an initiative of the Bahá'ís of Swindon. The Tranquillity Zone is a place where people can find time to rest and reflect on what is important in life. We find that people who attend the Tranquillity Zone return many times and recommend it to their friends. They are touched by the sincere environment of love and friendship and this is what attracts people back. More than 2,500 people have attended the Tranquillity Zone in Swindon. Seven sessions are held each fortnight, with an extra lunchtime session every Friday at 1 p.m.

In Swindon, the Tranquillity Zone is presented to the public in two ways:

• As an outreach service, when we visit different community groups, businesses, clinics, hospitals, and more recently schools, to offer them a way of dealing with increasing levels of stress. Some of the groups we have visited so far include: an organization to help people overcome their drug problems, where regular monthly sessions are held; the local hospital; an AIDs advice centre for victims and their families; centres and clinics which cater for people with mental health problems; a nursing home; a centre for the disabled; a staff support centre for hospital staff; family centres; businesses and schools. We have also run Tranquillity Zones for staff at Swindon Borough Council.

• As a service open to all members of the public: These sessions for the public have been held in a leisure centre venue in Swindon town centre for the past three years. It houses swimming baths, a gym and a women's health centre and its rooms are rented by practitioners of alternative medicines.

Of course these approaches are not the only ways in which Tranquillity Zones can be used. Each community has to consult and find its own way. We have heard good reports of some places where Zones are held in people's homes by Bahá'ís. Whatever the approach, the aim is the same: to offer a service of spiritual development and enrichment to all who participate.

Promoting the Tranquillity Zone

The local and regional media will be interested in the Tranquillity Zone venture but it requires care to present it to them properly (see the information on contacting the media). Remember that your media can be print (newspapers), radio and television.

You can also generate your own leaflets and posters and distribute them. Useful phrasing for these includes:

> The Tranquillity Zone . . . Discover an oasis of calm and well-being for your body, mind and soul. The Tranquillity Zone is a multi-sensory experience of peace and serenity, held in a candlelit setting. It is a place of rest, reflection and spiritual refuelling, with inspiring words and soothing music. A welcome escape from the pressures of life.

Don't forget to include a contact telephone number and e-mail address, and to mention who the organizing body is. You might like to include the URL for this Website <www.tranquillity-zone.org.uk> as well.

The friends distribute these leaflets around the town and in public centres such as libraries, public information centres, music shops and anywhere else where people agree to display the poster.

If the Tranquillity Zone is being held for or in association with another organization, speak to them about joint publicity for it. Two sets of resources are better than one.

Finally, regarding the media, don't forget you have two chances to publicize the Tranquillity Zone: before and after. While before is better in generating interest for this time, more publicity after will help familiarize people with the Tranquillity Zone concept and make things easier the next time it is held. Why not do both? If the press send a photographer or the radio do an interview, that is very good but, if not, you can submit a press release afterwards reporting on the Tranquillity Zone and its success.

Contacting the Media

The Tranquillity Zone can provide many opportunities for local and even national media coverage. Ideally, a community should appoint its own press liaison officer, who can set up and sustain regular contact with the local press, radio and television. It is important to know:

- How to make the initial contact
- When to call
- Who to approach
- What to say
- How to compile press releases
- How to maintain contact

HOW TO MAKE INITIAL CONTACT

Initial contact can be made by phone to the news desk of the paper/radio station/TV newsroom. Introduce yourself to the reporter and explain briefly about the event, in this case the Tranquillity Zone. If the reporter is interested, arrange to meet with him or her and in that way you can begin to build up a good relationship. If he/she doesn't appear very interested, say that you will send him further details. They like you to make the effort. And if there isn't much happening news-wise that day or week, you could end up on the front page . . .

WHEN TO CALL

Always give the reporter plenty of notice – at least a week or two – before the event, so that he can put it in his diary and possibly arrange for a photographer to come along. If the paper is a daily, try to avoid calling early in the morning, as reporters will be tied up with the day's paper. Try to call after lunch, if possible, when the reporter will have more time to talk to you.

WHO TO APPROACH

First of all, tell the reporter that you are running an event which will be of interest locally. If the reporter shows interest, you can give him/her the details over the phone, or better still, send a press release – or take it into the office where you can meet the reporter and have eye-to-eye contact.

NEWSWORTHY ITEMS

Newspapers are always looking for local stories to fill their pages. It doesn't have to be something major. Anything happening in the community is of interest and something like the Tranquillity Zone will capture the attention of many reporters because they know that their readers will be interested in the service.

If a report doesn't get included in your paper, just keep trying.

Why not invite your local reporter to a Tranquillity Zone and ask him/her to do a report on the experience? He/she could also invite the photographer and you could end up getting big exposure for the project. Be audacious!

Of course there are many other ways of attracting the interest of the local press and we should never give up.

PRESS RELEASES

Don't worry too much about the structure of your press releases. It is almost certain that reporters will rewrite the story into their own style anyway. The most important thing is to make sure that all the relevant details are included. Here are a few useful tips:

- Always use full names and not initials
- Include addresses of venues, dates, times
- Always include your own daytime telephone number or the number of a Bahá'í who will be available to talk to the press during office hours
- Give some suggestions for photo opportunities
- Keep the press release fairly concise

From the media's point of view, the important thing is the news angle: this is not a publicity puff for the Bahá'í Faith. The press will not wish to feel they are being used as a publicity vehicle for the Faith but they will be happy to carry news items about people or events in their area, who happen to be Bahá'ís.

You will find an example of a press release on the Tranquillity Zone below. It is a good idea to include a few explanatory sentences at the end about the Bahá'í Faith but it's almost inevitable that the reporter will ask you anyway.

How to Maintain Contact

- Once you have made initial contact with your local media, it is vital that you keep in regular touch. You should try to offer at least one news item a month.

- Don't be shy about regularly contacting the newspaper, radio station or TV. They always like to know what is going on and have pages and airtime to fill!

- Don't be disappointed if the story isn't used. Sometimes they don't have space or perhaps they consider that it won't be of much interest to people.

Success with the media is all about persevering and keeping them regularly informed.

PRESS RELEASE: TRANQUILLITY ZONE

The demands of life today seem to come at us from every direction, as we are constantly under pressure at work and at home. But help is at hand, thanks to a service called the Tranquillity Zone.

The Tranquillity Zone is a unique oasis of calm for the body, mind and soul and an uplifting experience of peace and well-being. It can be held in any kind of room which is then transformed into a beautiful candlelit setting, adorned with fresh flowers and drapes – a kind of spiritual changing rooms! Participants relax in large comfortable cushions and listen to inspiring words and soothing music. A welcome escape from the pressures of life. The Tranquillity Zone is an initiative and service of the local Bahá'í Community.

Spokesman Jane Smith said: 'It is a multisensory experience of peace and serenity, where participants can enjoy a break from their busy lives and enjoy some uplifting music and words.

'And as they reflect on nourishing the spiritual side of life and nurturing a sense of well-being, it can help them cope with the increasing levels of stress in our hectic world.'

Entry is free. Sessions last 40 minutes and will be held at . . . Refreshments will be served. For further information contact Jane Smith on (daytime telephone number).

You might like to add this background information on the Bahá'í Faith as a separate sheet:

The Bahá'í Faith is an independent world religion, founded almost 160 years ago. Bahá'ís believe that its founder Bahá'u'lláh (1817–92) is the Messenger of God for today. The central message of the Bahá'í Faith is unity – that there is only one God, that the human race is one family and that all the world's religions are one, representing one changeless and eternal Faith of God, and expressions of one single, unfolding Divine Plan. Among the central principles of the Bahá'í Faith are: the oneness of God; the oneness of religion and the oneness of humanity; the equality of men and women; the elimination of prejudice; the elimination of the extremes of wealth and poverty; the independent investigation of

Truth; universal education; the harmony of science and religion; a world commonwealth of nations and a universal auxiliary language. The Bahá'í Faith is now the world's second most widespread religion after Christianity.

Suggested Readings for the Tranquillity Zone

A suggestion for the start of the Tranquillity Zone session:

Close the door for just a while
And seek the peace within.
Shut out the world and all its noise
And let the silence in.
Close your ears for just a while
Until you only hear
That still small voice that whispers
All is well, for you are here.

Or you could start with the favourite Bahá'í prayer:

Blessed is the spot, and the house, and the place, and the city, and the heart, and the mountain, and the refuge, and the cave, and the valley, and the land, and the sea, and the island, and the meadow where mention of God hath been made, and His praise glorified. *Bahá'u'lláh*

And/or a quotation:

O my friend! Listen with heart and soul to the songs of the spirit and cherish them as thine own eyes. *Bahá'u'lláh*

Reprinted with the permission of the National Spiritual Assembly of the United Kingdom www.tranquillity-zone.org.uk

Tranquillity Hour
Katherine and Michael Hainsworth

What can you do when you have just moved into a new town and a small home? Newly-weds Katherine and Michael Hainsworth found a way to hold regular devotional meetings.

We knew that a devotional meeting could be put together in a variety of ways but looking at the Tranquillity Zone website was a good place to start. Impressive and successful but it made us realize that we were too few in numbers, with too little money, we didn't know enough people to fill a small hall and not nearly enough white sheets to create a Swindon-style Tranquillity Zone. Considering our situation it was evident that we first needed to make some friends! We had moved into our flat at the beginning of the year and our conversation so far with any of our neighbours hadn't developed beyond 'Good morning/afternoon/evening'.

We decided to start with a coffee morning. We invited all the neighbours we at least knew by sight and with whom we could link a front door with the face. We had no idea what the response would be.

Six neighbours were invited and six came to the coffee morning. We were happy they had accepted the invitation. In our small living room we managed to welcome and just about seat our guests, from a newborn to an 85 year old. The range was quite impressive.

Following the coffee morning we no longer felt like the alien newcomers to the neighbourhood. If they didn't find us pleasant people, our neighbours could at least trust we made good coffee. There was an ease and familiarity that gave us confidence to start our 'devotional meetings'.

We delivered a simple invitation via the same letter-boxes. We called our devotional meeting a 'Tranquillity Hour'. The invitation read:

Tranquillity Hour: an antidote to the stresses of modern living using a combination of music and the Bahá'í Writings.

We gave a list of four dates; the same weekday, every other week.

One neighbour thanked us but declined the invitation politely, stating on a note that she wasn't interested in Bahá'í. This was left on our doorstep with a wrapped gift of shower gel. Another declined in person, some we didn't hear from but, impressively, two showed an interest; the 85 year old and a housewife.

Why is it that with all the Bahá'í writings we have, to choose but a few which are appropriate can be a long and anxious task? In a way, I guess we were just that little bit nervous. It was no longer about serving a good cup of coffee but introducing to people the words of the latest Manifestation of God.

Our two neighbours turned up and we had a lovely evening. The music volume was increased/decreased as smoothly as the stereo would permit. The readings were brief and not too heavy. We made sure all attending received a printed copy to take home with them. The 85 year old seemed to enjoy the atmosphere and appreciate the company. She fell asleep during the readings and then chatted about anything and everything over the refreshments.

Our other neighbour follows pantheism but because

she has a young family and a working husband she doesn't get much of a chance to reflect on her spirituality and these tranquillity hours give her this opportunity.

We have more or less kept the evenings going. We continue to give out invitations. This has now branched out to friends of other local Bahá'ís, local people with whom we have had a casual 'spiritual' conversation. These include an acupuncturist, a beautician and a student. The programme remains simple: 20 minutes of readings and music then a good hour of chatting, frequently about the Faith.

The attendance has ranged from 11 (five non-Bahá'ís) to just the two of us. We never cancel the evening just because we are the only two. By regularly offering the devotional meetings, we have an act of service that is open to all. This gives us something to which we can always invite people.

The numbers may often be low but the benefits are immeasurable. The fact that we are aligning ourselves to the guidance of the Universal House of Justice is empowering and never makes it a waste of time.

Devotional Meetings in Cities

Tranquillity in the City
Mary Sarooshi

From September 2001, the two London Bahá'í communities of Kensington & Chelsea and Westminster have been holding regular Tranquillity Zones, demonstrating that it is possible to find peace, quiet and spiritual nourishment in a busy metropolis.

The Tranquillity Zone is a unique oasis of calm for the body, mind and soul as well as an uplifting experience of peace and well-being. Our Tranquillity Zones are held in a large room in a public community centre/Christian girls' dormitory called the Maria Assumpta Centre. It is located just off the ever-bustling and highly popular High Street, Kensington.

The Tranquillity Zones are advertised through fliers, posters and word of mouth.

Before the start of each session the room is transformed into a beautiful sweet-smelling, candlelit setting, adorned with fresh flowers and drapes. Participants relax in large comfortable cushions and listen to inspiring words interspersed with soothing music. The selections come from the world's sacred writings. They are short, easily digestible readings which usually follow a given theme.

In the first year Tranquillity Zones were held on a weekly basis but they are now held on the first Saturday of every month.

The Tranquillity Zone Committee views the purpose of these 'Zones' to be two-fold: firstly, it is a service to our wider respective communities and secondly, if the opportunity arises, the Tranquillity Zone can act as a springboard for introducing our friends to the Bahá'í Faith.

The Tranquillity Zone Committee of Kensington & Chelsea and Westminster has taken on the responsibilities of organizing facilitators, setting up the environment before each session and advertising. The function of the facilitator is to organize the music and readings. The facilitator is asked to make a tape of the music so that it runs smoothly, without interruption, and to make a copy of the readings so that they can be used again. The only

prerequisite for being a facilitator is to attend one of our
Tranquillity Zones. The facilitator changes every month
in order to promote diversity in the way each session is
conducted and to encourage wider community support.

The Tranquillity Zone Committee hopes to get support from the Ruhi Institutes in our communities with the
aim that eventually the two groups will assist one another.

We feel the Tranquillity Zones are very successful.
On average, five to ten people attend each session. Most
of the participants are Bahá'ís but there are also some
'regulars' who are not Bahá'ís. We have had one declara-
tion so far as a result of our Tranquillity Zones. We have
maintained a comments book for participants to give
their views on the Tranquillity Zones and have been told
on numerous occasions that they are a welcome escape
from the pressures of life.

Two Moods in Manchester
Mieko Bond

Large Bahá'í communities in cities may have to provide
devotional meetings for a wide range of people, interests
and situations. In this English city the Bahá'ís offer two
types of devotional meetings, each with its own ambiance.

Devotionals take on two characters in the Manchester
community and the music is selected for the mood to be
achieved. One sort of devotional provides a sedate and
calming atmosphere and the music chosen reflects this. In
the other type, more fast-paced music creates a joyful
atmosphere. Each devotional revolves around a particular theme, such as 'parents', 'marriage', 'friendship' and
'love'. Sometimes themes for future devotionals are sug-

gested by those who attend. In addition, devotionals are prepared for special celebrations such as World Religion Day, when readings are selected to highlight the theme of the event.

Each devotional starts with a welcome and brief introduction to the devotionals and to the Bahá'í Faith. This is followed by music, which creates the appropriate atmosphere. Readers are selected from those who attend and several passages from the Bahá'í writings are read. This usually lasts about 20 to 25 minutes. After this is a period when anyone can offer prayers or read writings from any religious or other literature. The voluntary readings usually last around half an hour. The devotionals are then closed with singing prepared by the Manchester Bahá'í community choir.

At some devotionals special prayers are offered, for example healing prayers for the sick or prayers for world peace. Sometimes a breakfast is served at 10:00 a.m. before the devotional.

About a hundred people attend special occasion devotionals, while the regularly held devotionals attract between 20 and 50 people.

Devotional Meetings in Villages

The Seven Valleys: A Spiritual Odyssey
Wendi and Moojan Momen

We have lived in a small village of about 250 people since 1983. We have always held Bahá'í meetings and activities in our home, from Nineteen Day Feasts, holy day celebrations and Assembly meetings to firesides and junior youth camps. Once part of a larger Bahá'í community which had a Local Spiritual Assembly, when the boundaries were changed in 2001, our community was reduced to the two of us. But this also coincided with the beginning of the Five Year Plan so although we lost a community at one level, we gained a cluster, albeit a category 'C'.

At the second cluster meeting it was established that there were two or three study circles, children's classes and two regular devotional meetings in the cluster. It was agreed that we would try to increase the number of each of these by the next reflection meeting in a few months' time. As there was no study circle tutor available at our end of the county, nor any possibility of training one in the foreseeable future, and as we did not feel able to do children's classes ourselves, we agreed to start a regular devotional meeting.

With the boundary change, our 'new' community is so tiny that we can walk around its perimeter in about an hour. So we decided to walk around the whole community and view it from a new perspective while consulting on our devotional meeting. We both feel that what is missing in today's busy world is a sense of the mystical, as well as a lack of spirituality in general. We wanted our devotional meeting to evoke a sense of wonderment. We discussed various possibilities and as we were walking it struck us that we were making a journey around our community, seeking enlightenment, just as the soul makes its own journey. The journey of the soul reminded us of Bahá'u'lláh's great mystical work *The Seven Valleys* and our decision was made.

From there it was easy. For each devotional we chose readings on one of the Seven Valleys – search, love, knowledge and so on – from the Bahá'í and other sacred scriptures. Knowing we would have participants from many religious backgrounds, we tried to ensure that these readings were not only linked to the general theme but were meaningful to someone from the particular religious tradition represented. We also selected music of different types to complement the readings.

Because people are so used to coming to events in our house, we wanted to make this experience different to establish a feeling of reverence. Our friends are used to socializing in our house before any activity. However, for these gatherings we did not want to have them talking socially then suddenly try to hush them to create a devotional atmosphere. We have a rather small house with smallish rooms but we liked the idea of people 'entering' a sacred place, a place set apart. We are lucky to have a back room separate from the living room and it is there that people gather and chat before going into the devotional meeting in our living room. They are each given a copy of the programme and are asked if they will read a particular passage.

We decided to try to involve every sense in the devotional meeting, to make a complete experience for those who come. We had attended Tranquillity Zones in other communities and the Peace Tent at the Beijing UN Conference on Women and liked the ambiance created. However, we did not wish to spend huge amounts of time we do not have hanging drapes and moving furniture. So we tried to create a sort of sacred space, what we call a 'Tranquillity Zone without the curtains'. We bought lots of inexpensive tea light candles as well as larger ones in all sizes, some new candle holders and some scented oil. In a trial run, we placed these around the room and on a silk cloth in the centre of the floor along with fresh flowers.

Not having enough room to put chairs somewhere else, we arranged them as we had for other Bahá'í events, around the edges of the room. We burned the oil in a oil burner, lit the candles, turned off the lights, turned on the music – and the effect was magical.

We use the same basic idea for each Seven Valleys devotional, modifying it a bit in the summer when it stays light so late at night. To overcome the difficulty of reading by candlelight, we bought an old-fashioned candle holder in which we put a fairly stubby candle. This is passed to each reader in turn and seems to cast enough light. We also put the readings into very large print to help those of us with poor eyesight.

We never had any worries about who to invite. Over the years we have built up an invitation list of over 150 addresses of people we have met and who have come to a Bahá'í event or have shown some mild interest. We put everyone we meet on the list for a time – schoolteachers, the post lady, work colleagues, women from the women's club, magistrates, neighbours, delivery people, shopkeepers, the cattery owner, the gardener, people from the interfaith group, our cleaner (and her daughter), the masseuse, the hairdresser, doctors, dentists, people we meet on the train – and their friends too. We also have on the list a few Bahá'ís who live nearby. For other events we generally have about 40 people attending at any one time. We felt this would be too many for a devotional meeting – we wanted to keep the numbers to about 12 to 15. So we cut down the list to people who live very locally and this gave us 58 addresses. We made up simple invitations giving details of the first seven devotionals:

The Seven Valleys: A Spiritual Odyssey

'The stages that mark the wayfarer's journey from the abode of dust to the heavenly homeland are said to be seven. Some have called these Seven Valleys, and others, Seven Cities. And they say that until the wayfarer taketh leave of self, and traverseth these stages, he shall never reach to the ocean of nearness and union, nor drink of the peerless wine.'   *Bahá'u'lláh*

We invite you to a series of devotional meetings consisting of prayers, meditations, reading of scripture and music to assist our soul's journey towards God.

Then we listed the dates of all the devotionals arranged so far.

We walked around the area delivering those invitations we could and posted the others. We were surprised to get so many positive responses almost immediately. Our first Seven Valleys attracted 15 people, mostly non-Bahá'ís. Many people come regularly, new people attend every time and people ask to bring friends.

The devotional programme is read by those who attend. We try to give readings from the holy scriptures of each religion to a person from that religion. If we have no one from a particular tradition, we read that selection ourselves, especially if it includes difficult words. We also read the Bahá'í writings ourselves or ask other Bahá'ís to do so. People feel honoured to read something from their own holy writings – sometimes we find that a passage has already been memorized and that the person wants to say it by heart. The readings and music always seem to take exactly an hour and there is a brief period of personal meditation at the end.

When the lights eventually come up, we serve light refreshments of cold drinks, tea and coffee with cake, cheese and fresh fruit. People usually stay for another hour or so chatting, discussing some of the passages or asking about the Bahá'í Faith. We have Bahá'í literature available for guests to take home and we also tell them of other events taking place. Newcomers sign a guest book – especially those who have come with a friend for the first time, so that we can add their names to the invitation list.

We spend quite a bit of time putting the devotional programme together but feel it is time well spent. We enjoy the evening ourselves and know that people are moved by the beautiful words of the world's sacred scriptures.

Spiritual Keep Fit
Guitty Bonner

A lone Bahá'í living in a tiny village in the north of England hosts 'Spiritual Keep Fit':

The Allendale Assembly asked me to organize prayer meetings for us lot 'up the valley' in Tynedale during the winter months when it is more difficult for us to get together for Feasts. So I suggested that we up valley folk get together for devotionals open to all. I thought of a name and sent invitations out to the far-flung Bahá'ís in our area, mentioning that it was open for all to come.

At each meeting I experiment with readings from quite secular, but sympathetic, authors as well as from the major religions including our own, of course, and play music between the selections. Those who come enjoy the 'array' of readings and music. Although at first some of the Bahá'ís still thought in terms of our meetings being a

Nineteen Day Feast substitute, gradually we have come to understand the significance of the devotional as a core activity of this plan.

Neiafu, Vava'u
Don Blanks

In Neiafu, Vava'u, Tonga we have yet to multiply our devotional meetings. We still have our weekly devotions in a central location. However, because of our on-going study circles and firesides we are getting a steady stream of seekers to our devotional meetings. To a certain degree this has changed the way that they are run.

Each family takes a turn preparing the programme. This means that each week there is a slightly different flavour to the devotional meeting. For example, there will be some Samoan the night that our Samoan/ Tongan family presents the programme. The basic ingredients consist of a lot of singing, prayers by every age, recitation of the holy writings from memory and reading from the scriptures of the Bahá'í Faith. Occasionally a short talk will be given. Several families like to bring readings from other holy scriptures, especially from Christianity.

The devotions take place at the little Bahá'í Centre. We sit on the floor in a large circle and those coming in late can sit at the back. Interestingly enough, Neiafu has pretty well conquered the 'start on time' problem. This is unusual in the Pacific islands! There are usually between 30 and 40 people present, though that number can swell to 50 on occasion.

While we have yet to get any of the friends to have devotions in their own homes and to invite neighbours

and friends, we do have a tradition of family prayers and
devotions in the family. Most families in Vava'u, Bahá'í or
Christian, will gather in the morning for time together.
This has caused the friends to be a little hesitant to reach
out to the wider community. However, we have eight
seekers currently participating in our three local study
circles and have had four declarations from study circles
so far. Most of the seekers who have declared had
become regular participants in weekly devotions before
they joined the Bahá'í community.

Individual Initiatives

The 'Long Healing Prayer' Musical Devotional Meeting
Allen Tyrone Johnson and Rose Wendel

Allen Tyrone Johnson, a young Bahá'í musician, under-
took a year-long travel teaching trip around the United
States offering each of more than 200 communities an
opportunity to attend and participate in his 'Long
Healing Prayer' musical devotional. Allen sings the long
healing prayer and accompanies himself on the guitar.
He asks those present to join in singing some of the
verses. Many have been deeply touched by his presenta-
tion. Here is his story:

I declared myself a Bahá'í in 1990. When we prayed we
closed our eyes and sat quietly. In 1992 I started Project
Melody, the goal of which was to 'set to music the verses
and the divine words so that they may be sung with
soul-stirring melody in the Assemblies and gatherings,
and that the hearts of the listeners may become tumultuous and rise towards the Kingdom of Abhá in

supplication and prayer'[10] and to create music which was 'as a ladder for your souls, a means whereby they may be lifted up unto the realm on high'.[11]

On the anniversary of the Birth of the Báb 2002 we were having an intensive Ruhi training weekend at the Bahá'í Centre in Kansas City, Missouri. So instead of attending the celebration with the Kansas City Metro community, we had a study circle celebration.

We had to put something together so I suggested that we do the 'Long Healing Prayer' with music in a participatory way.

The facilitators consulted and then asked the group. We decided we would do it, on the understanding that if people wanted to leave they could 'because this is a long prayer'. We had our celebration, which lasted for about 90 minutes, including the devotional.

Immediately after the prayer a Bahá'í from Overland Park asked if I would come to his community to do a similar devotional. I agreed. That evening the 'Long Healing Prayer' devotional meeting was born.

Within about one week we had a cluster meeting at the Bahá'í Centre and we all made a pledge about what we were going to contribute to the plan. Since focus was given to children's classes, study circles and devotional meetings, and to 'advance the process of entry by troops', I pledged to 'follow through with the invitation within the next six months and do one devotional meeting with the "Long Healing Prayer"'.

Next I received an invitation to do some music for a youth retreat in Overland Park. That evening I decided to try the 'Long Healing Prayer' again and that night we had a new soul enlist under the banner of the Promised One. She grew up with the daughter of a Bahá'í family and knew about the Faith but had never had that 'feeling' of being 'emotionally moved'.

That evening was full of inspiration to me and others. Bahá'u'lláh says, 'O Son of Man! For everything there is a sign'[12] and I took that experience as a sign. I had to struggle with myself to believe them when the participants told me, 'This was great.' I took that as another 'sign' to really try to see the value in this. For me it was just music, it seemed like no big deal. I have always done music.

That night the mother of the hosting family said to me, 'You need to share this with other communities.' Several weekends later she had made all the preparations. Thus her family and I drove to Hayes, Kansas, to do our first formal devotional meeting.

Everything was taken care of: they drove, the food was prepared, lodging was provided. All I needed to do was show up and do the devotional. We arrived at the home where the devotional meeting was to be held and discovered that I knew the hosts from California when we had all lived there about 11 years before.

We talked for three hours catching up and then consulted about travelling to other communities and offering this devotional meeting. The woman of the family was the travel teaching coordinator for the Central States where I live and that consultation was vital to the success of the project.

After our consultation we had dinner and then held the devotional. Again that night the experience was beyond words.

When I returned home, the Central Regional Bahá'í Council wrote to all other Regional Bahá'í Councils offering me as a travel teacher using the 'Long Healing

Prayer' for a 'Musical Devotional Meeting'. I departed on my travels on 11 January 2003.

To advertise the meetings, local Bahá'ís use word of mouth, fliers, email, phone and newspapers. In addition, the participants themselves email and call other family and friends in the areas I am to visit.

On the day, we arrange the chairs in the room in a circle. On average, 11 people come to each meeting, with the largest attendance being 80 and the smallest two. The programme is about an hour and half long with an introduction of approximately ten minutes, 40 to 50 minutes of music and questions at the end for the rest of the time.

In the first four months of my travels I held 115 'Long Healing Prayer Musical Devotional Meetings' attended by some 1,100 people. So far, seven people have declared their belief in Bahá'u'lláh.

Prayers with Friends and Neighbours
Linda Dye

Following considerable study of the directions from the House of Justice concerning the establishment of devotional gatherings, children's classes and study circles, my husband and I thought, prayed and trusted a lot! Just what is it we two senior citizens could do in response to the guidance of the Universal House of Justice to the Bahá'í world?

Remembering a comment by one of our Auxiliary Board members that 'eventually, there will be devotional gatherings and child education in every block in every city', the understanding took hold – that this is where all the action is!

The area where we live is rural agricultural and termed a 'bedroom community' since most people work away from their acreage during the week to make a livelihood and work all weekend on their land's most prominent crop in preparation for market. Therefore few of us know our neighbours in any way unless we encounter them at a business meeting dealing with the production and marketing of crops – not really an environment lending itself to becoming 'friends'. Most people in the area are Christian-based in their basic philosophy. However, most of the time, religion is a subject that is avoided in discussions. As a result, it has been quite a challenge to invite our neighbours to devotional gatherings in our home but one that has given us confirmation of divine assistance time and again.

Our first devotional gathering was the first Saturday evening in August 2002 and we have held one each month since – same day, same time each month. We began with lots of prayers for guidance and assistance in making a list of friends and neighbours. On the list were even folks we knew only slightly but we thought just might welcome the invitation. We try to invite about 15 to 20 people each month. We repeat some invitations but those who do not respond or attend are replaced on the list after a while. We welcome those who do attend to bring others who may appreciate the experience. Attendance most often is seven to ten people. Two of those come very regularly, others occasionally, and often someone new comes. The original attendees still return often. There is a good mix of both Bahá'ís and non-Bahá'ís attending.

We invite people by speaking to them in person or over the telephone and/or we send written invitations at least two weeks ahead of the event. The heading on the invitations vary and are occasionally 'event' oriented. One time it said: 'Please come and share in a spirit of loving friendship, a brief respite from the world's turmoil – with other friends and neighbours of many paths of Faith'. On another occasion we wrote: 'Devotions – Prayers – In Memory and Recognition of Our Seven Astronauts'. On yet another we stated: 'You are warmly invited to share an evening of Prayer and Devotion with Friends and Neighbours of Many Faiths and Spiritual Paths'.

We choose prayers and readings from various sources – all relating to God, the spirit and moral truths. We ask our guests to bring something they especially like and feel comfortable sharing if they wish. Some bring poetry or quotable quotes from famous and not so famous people and we provide readings from the holy books of various faiths. Also, we have gift copies of *Seekers' Prayers* (a short selection of Bahá'í prayers) and *The Interfaith Prayer Book*, which our guests nearly always take home and we lend them our own books including *A World of Faith* which was prepared for the Interfaith Council and distributed at the Salt Lake City 2002 Winter Olympics. Additionally, we provide sets of two and three pages of beautiful but short and meaningful readings and invite the attendees to take them home – and they do! Each page has one selection from the Bahá'í prayers or texts along with others from various sources including Native American traditions. All these pieces of literature are put out on a large coffee table and people look them over and select what they wish. To us, sharing the truths to be found in other faiths and spiritual readings is teaching the oneness of religion in a different way than we have in the past. We find the non-Bahá'ís really respond very positively to this approach.

We occasionally use soft, soothing instrumental background music but not always. When we do use it, it is set to play continuously during the readings. Sometimes there will be a small candle burning and fresh flowers on the coffee table but not always. We try to vary the environment as well as the readings so as to avoid any idea of rituals.

We welcome children and two children have attended more than once with their mothers. They too participate in selecting readings from the available materials or bring something they wish to share. They are a part of the group, not set aside.

The devotional portion of the evening lasts for about 30 to 40 minutes, sometimes less depending on the spirit and mood of the group. No one is assigned to read and those who wish to read do so when they feel comfortable. Very light refreshments (coffee, tea, cookies) are served following devotions.

We try hard to avoid having a fireside! We answer any questions briefly and invite those wishing to know more about the Bahá'í Faith to another evening planned especially for that kind of activity. We stress that the purpose of the devotional gathering is to soothe the soul of those present and to further bond friendships with our God and each other.

Everyone is more relaxed following the readings and we are grateful that the gatherings are such a success. They seem to have a profound effect on people. A friend and neighbour who attends regularly recently brought her two sisters and her ten year old child, who more than once has willingly participated by selecting readings. This friend always comments about how she 'so looks forward to these evenings'. 'They really lift my spirits,' she says.

'They are really spiritual sustenance and seem to go deep into my being.' She recently read *Release the Sun* and, in her words, 'loves it'. The two sisters recently told us that in the 1980s following graduation from college, they had toured Europe, staying in hospices. While in London someone had given them *Paris Talks*! One sister said, 'I love that book! Even the paper it is printed on has such a lovely feel.' All three of them have been awed by the evening's experiences and since attending have hung in their homes a plaque quoting the Golden Rule as it is presented in the scriptures of each major religion. What gifts – to see others expand their spiritual consciousness!

So touched by the devotional gatherings was one man that when his mother passed away he asked the Bahá'ís to assist him with the preparations for the funeral and to do a graveside service for her. Of course we were honoured to do so. Everyone in attendance spoke most kindly about the beauty of the readings and the loveliness of the simple service.

Will our devotional meetings lead others to a deeper study of the Faith? Who knows? All we can do is our best and let Bahá'u'lláh guide those whom He wishes.

Community-Sponsored Devotionals

Spiritual TEA
Judith Fienieg and Robert Weinberg

The London communities of Southwark and Lambeth have created a special monthly Sunday devotional meeting in a public library in Peckham. Called 'Spiritual TEA (Tranquillity, Enlightenment, Awakening)', its purpose is 'to refresh and gladden the spirit'.

The room itself is an unusual one, of modern design. Painted all in white, it is shaped like an organic pod/igloo/UFO with a skylight that opens like butterfly wings. The room is very different from rooms usually found in libraries and lends itself to the creation of a spiritual environment within it.

The idea of using 'tea' came from a young Bahá'í designer. His thought was to attract people into the devotional through an imaginative invitation and that after the devotional people would spend time together over a cup of tea and biscuits. The poster and invitation card show a cup of tea with its steam rising into the shape of a halo.

The programme consists of Bahá'í readings and music. Much attention is given to beauty, with candles and flowers creating a calming ambience with appropriate fragrance and relaxing music. Flowers are offered to participants when the programme is over.

Each of the Spiritual TEAs have led to further discussions about the Faith with visitors. Interestingly, some people wander up to the devotional room after the programme has finished to join in the teatime discussion.

Prayers for Peace
Arthur Weinberg

As the Universal House of Justice has asked that devotional meetings be 'open to all', one needs firstly to ensure there will be an audience for the meeting. In Canterbury, our community has always been actively involved with 'like-minded organizations' and are committee members on the United Nations Association, Canterbury Interfaith and the Multicultural Association. I have also run four courses on 'Comparative Religion' for U3A (University of the Third Age). By being involved with these organizations we now have a mailing list of over a hundred people and so we are able to draw on these resources for invitations.

We arrange two different types of meetings. The first is a small group of 10 to 12 guests in our own home. Numbers are restricted owing to accommodation and also to people we know personally who can be invited because of particular shared interests. The second meeting is a large 'public' meeting always arranged to celebrate a holy day – Naw-Rúz, particularly, or the Birth of Bahá'u'lláh. For this a hall is booked, occasionally a small church hall – provided the religious denomination knows exactly what we are doing and has no objections – but we usually use the Friends' Meeting House as we have established a close relationship with the Quakers over the years.

The format for both meetings is the same – a programme of readings and music with a particular theme. We prefer shorter readings as this helps with concentration, about 12 usually, and these are interspersed with short pieces of music, roughly between every three or four readings. The readings are taken from the scriptures of all the world religions but occasionally we might use the words of a philosopher or great leader if appropriate. For a programme on peace we selected our readings from *The Peace Bible* and this included Martin Luther King and Mahatma Gandhi. The programme is typed out and photocopied so that each participant can follow the readings and, more importantly, have them to take away afterwards for re-reading. One non-Bahá'í friend came up to me afterwards and said that the little programme booklet would now become her 'bible' for daily readings.

At the meeting in our home, the chairs are arranged around the room and in the centre is a small table with a flower arrangement and possibly candles. These are not always used because some members of other religious traditions are not very happy with candles as they are associated with rituals alien to them. Lighting is subdued, with two reading lamps at opposite ends of the room. Because of this only two readers are asked to do the whole programme as they are seated next to the lamps. As visitors arrive they are seated and when we are ready to start, the main light is switched off and the music is started. The programme ends again with music followed by a short silence and the centre light is switched on. Comments on the readings are encouraged and then refreshments are served.

At the public meeting, the chairs are arranged in rows, preferably in a semicircle around a central table holding flowers. If the invitation contains an RSVP and people actually do respond, we can put out a suitable number of chairs as we do not want to have to hurriedly put out extra chairs at the last minute or, on the other hand, welcome about 30 people to a hall with a hundred chairs so that they begin to sit in small pockets, usually at the back. These meetings attract between 20 and 50 participants each time.

The invitation to the public meeting states that refreshments will be served half an hour before the start of the programme so that people can come in and meet and so that the hosts can have hot drinks ready and not have to jump up to put on kettles during the devotional or have to do a lot of clearing up later. As the room is usually light (daytime meetings) different readers are chosen, usually from the visitors who are happy to read from their own scriptures.

The choice of music is very important as this sets the whole tone and atmosphere of the meeting. The theme of the readings can be echoed in the music and a few suggestions are listed below. If using a short piece between readings, this should not be more than five minutes long. We have experimented with long pieces which can be played for the duration of the programme, where these are faded out and brought back whenever required. For this purpose the piece must be consistently calm and of a similar mood as we do not want to be confronted with a sudden loud chord or crash of percussion as the volume is slowly raised again after a reading.

Short pieces to suit a particular theme:

Spring
Grieg: Morning, from Peer Gynt
Last Spring
Mendelssohn: Spring Song
Sinding: Rustle of Spring
Ravel: Lever du jour (Daphnis and Chloe)

The Good Shepherd
Bach: Sheep may safely graze
Rutter: The Lord is my Shepherd
Canteloube: Bailero (Songs of the Auvergne)

Meditation
Barber: Adagio
Satie: Gymopedie I
Faure: Pavane
Any selection from 'Adagio' compilations

Long pieces suitable for fading in and out:
Vaughan-Williams: The Lark Ascending (14 minutes)
Mahler: Adagietto from 5th Symphony (9 minutes)
Brahms: Symphony No. 3, 4rd movement (6½ minutes)

Film music can be very useful:

John Williams: *Schindler's List, Saving Private Ryan* (Hymn
for the Fallen)
John Barry: *Out of Africa* (main theme), *Beyondness of
Things, Dances with Wolves*

Tranquillity in an Ancient City
Anne Maund

Chester is a walled city in the north of England with a
long history. Founded as the Roman legionary fortress
and naval base of Deva in 79 AD, it became an important Saxon town in the early 10th century, was a military
centre in the Middle Ages and became a cathedral city
in 1541. Today it hosts a small but innovative Bahá'í
community.

'You are invited to experience a relaxing, serene and calm
environment – a Tranquillity Zone. Try this peaceful
meditation just by relaxing with soothing words and
music. The session will last about 20 minutes, with
refreshments afterwards.'

Thus read the poster advertising the fortnightly
Tranquillity Zones of the Chester Bahá'í community at
the Blacon Community Centre. Each session was open to
the general public and had a different theme, such as

'Love', 'Remembrance', 'Contentment'. We shared a mixture of readings from the Bahá'í writings, other faiths, some poetry and sentiments.

The 'Remembrance' occasion was especially poignant because the 'regulars' had been told about it the week before and were invited to bring along a photograph or memento of a loved one who had passed on or of anyone special they would like to think of during the session.

We always had an opportunity to chat afterwards in the intimate setting of the floral, candlelit gazebo and take refreshment together. We began to get to know our regular visitors and new people too, who soon opened up and were ready to talk about themselves and spiritual ideas. The Bahá'í Faith was warmly received.

When it became impossible to keep the venue, the Tranquillity Zone had to close. However, the Chester friends were inspired to organize further Tranquillity Zones stemming from the relationship formed with a health and community worker who had helped organize some of the finances for all these events.

One session took place in the Blacon Project Youth Club where the 'Changing Rooms Team' really had to surpass itself to transform a very dingy and abused location – a large breezeblock and corrugated iron hut. Things improved once the lights were out – every scene is charmed by candlelight! Here the youth workers themselves were subjected to our charms and Bahá'í's writings. They felt very 'chilled' at the end of it and planned to try something along these lines with the youth who attend the club.

Two Bahá'ís sensitively handled a delicate situation when they took the theme of 'Love' to a women's refuge in Chester. Not having had a chance to meet the users of the service beforehand meant they had to tread carefully in an emotionally charged atmosphere. The Tranquillity experience was very well received.

One of the important effects of hosting the Tranquillity Zones was that because everyone in the community contributed something, it was a great point of unity for the Bahá'ís of Chester.

Devotional Meetings for Young People

Youth Devotionals in Ireland
Ian Hamilton

I began hosting devotional evenings in my own home in answer to the call of the House of Justice to further the clustering process. Before I began, I consulted with the assistant to the Auxiliary Board for my area about what was best and we decided I should hold the meeting weekly.

The devotional evening is primarily aimed at youth and although I don't stop older youth (i.e. adults) from coming, the average age of those who attend is 24 years. I invite both Bahá'ís and non-Bahá'ís and some enquirers have, in fact, attended. So far, however, it has worked out that it is mainly Bahá'ís who come.

The devotional programme follows the same format every night. There is a round of prayers or readings by either all or some of the participants. So far we have only used Bahá'í prayers and scriptures, with the participants themselves choosing whatever they want to read.

Then, and this is the good part, I play a CD of some selected music. Just songs that move me or that I really like and find uplifting. I have used every sort of music apart from pop, which doesn't appeal to me, so I just leave it out.

As the CD plays, all the participants draw a picture, write something or just do something artistic that they are moved to do by hearing the prayers, readings and the music. The drawings and pictures are going to be displayed at our next reflection meeting, so something that was started by the clustering process is now giving back to it.

The devotional usually lasts 10 to 15 minutes and refreshments are served during the 'artistic' period.

The programme seems to be successful with people coming back a second time and attending other Bahá'í activities as well. However, I am meeting again with the assistant to the Auxiliary Board to assess the programme and see where to go next.

Children Create Peace in the School TZ
Ephrat Miller

After a visit to a Tranquillity Zone, the first in Havant, I was keen to share the experience, so I approached the Headteacher of the school where I work.

My school is situated in a socially disadvantaged area of Hampshire where unemployment is high and drug and alcohol problems rife. The Head is always keen to broaden the children's range of experiences, so when I described a TZ he was willing to give it a go with years 5 and 6 children [10 and 11 years old]. He offered support but asked me not to give it a religious angle, as this is a 'delicate subject'.

So I was left with the flowers, candles, music and scents but no readings until a colleague suggested a wonderful idea: that the children should write about a chosen theme and it would be their offerings we would read at the TZ. I asked the children to write a short sentence on the virtue of courtesy, respect or friendship. I only needed to make very few minor adjustments to their contributions to make the readings flow a little more naturally. I also added some short poems on the same themes for extra depth and variety.

As this was new to the children I asked their teachers to give me a few minutes to brief and prepare them before the session. Then in groups of 15, the children entered the Tranquillity Zone, a room decorated with beautiful flowers, lit by the warm glow of burning candles and filled with the soft, soothing sound of music. The next two hours were magical. In one group after another, the children sat quietly, listening to their thoughts being read out to them, thoughts that were so moving and so hopeful!

The feedback from the children was overwhelmingly touching; some said that it made them think again about what friendship meant, two children said it made them remember their (departed) grandfathers, others said it was like religion and one girl it said it made her feel that she was somebody!

The fame of the Tranquillity Zone spread throughout the school so that a month later, when another TZ was being organized, a number of staff asked if they could come too. Unable to attend the first TZ owing to a prior engagement, the Head made sure he was present for the second one. He was so impressed by the children's reactions and their relaxed respectful attitude as well as the TZ environment that he has now decided to integrate it into the school's timetable. The plan is to organize a TZ once or twice per half term and the children wishing to attend will register for a chosen session.

At the end of the second TZ a member of staff walked up to me and, with eyes filled with tears, embraced me saying she had remembered all the people in her life, present and absent, 'sending them her love'. Another said the following day that the 'feeling of well-being continued throughout the evening'. But above all, it was the children's instinctive and intuitive openness and receptiveness that made it all so rewarding and worthwhile.

First published in *Bahá'í Journal UK*, February 2001. Reprinted with the permission of the author and the National Spiritual Assembly of the Bahá'ís of the United Kingdom.

Inner City Regeneration
Ian Holland and Steve Thompson

It was poignant that the first ever Tranquillity Zone in Stoke-on-Trent was held in the most deprived ward in the city. The venue was the disused shell of an old supermarket in a run-down shopping precinct at the heart of one of the largest public housing schemes ever constructed in the United Kingdom. A few months before, a youth programme had commandeered the building as part of a project that sought to reduce spiralling neighbourhood crime. The Tranquillity Zone idea buddied-up with the youth initiative as a way of offering the young people, as well as members of that community, the prospect of experiencing something a little bit different, maybe spiritual – the chance to sit back, in complete peace and ease, and reflect for a few precious moments on their inner thoughts and to let their troubles and stresses wash away. Judging by the comments that were subsequently made in the visitor's book located at the Zone, it touched many people in a very special way that day.

The Zone was organized by members of a Personal Development Study Circle following the 'Ruhi method' (book 1). It consisted of members of the Bahá'í communities of Stoke, Stafford and Congleton, together with some neighbours and friends of the Bahá'ís of Stafford. Part of the development process included the organization of a community project. A Tranquillity Zone seemed like the perfect venture.

One of the study circle members had contacts with a regeneration project in the Bentilee area of Stoke. The people of Bentilee were approached with the idea of creating a Tranquillity Zone within the derelict supermarket. Community leaders and regeneration project staff were receptive to the idea, so the detailed planning began. Invitations were designed, printed and issued to the community and regeneration project staff to distribute.

The evening immediately before the event, a Friday night in February 2002, the group set to work. Within three hours the interior of the old supermarket premises had been transformed into an oasis of calm. Nothing short of a complete internal 'make-over' was effected. Project staff, community members and young people who knew the building were mesmerised when they arrived the following morning.

A central focal point was constructed out of a coffee table and some crates covered with flame-retardant material, with candles (some floating, some in holders) and vases of fresh flowers. A member of the Bahá'í Community of Macclesfield had contributed a generous quantity of materials that were used to create an enclosure of cream white to soften and disguise the graffitied surrounding walls and ceilings to make the Zone more welcoming and homely. Rugs were laid and the ropey old furniture that had been recently gifted to the youth project was covered with embroidered throws. Low intensity electric lighting was also added, both for effect and to provide the people who were to read quotations over inspiring background music with enough light to see what to read. The overall effect was stunning.

The Zone was run over four separate sessions in the course of a whole day. Each session was based on a specific theme: 'Peace', 'Hope', 'Life and Soul' and finally 'Youth'. Around 20 readings were selected to match each theme, taken from a wide variety of religious sources including the Bahá'í writings. Calm and tranquil music drawn from many traditions, from classical to modern trance, was compiled for use. The music served as background for each session. Each theme was designed to last for 35 to 40 minutes and an hour separated each programme.

Before each session the guests were welcomed in an outer area, where they were introduced to the Tranquillity Zone concept and given a description of what was to happen. They were then guided into the Tranquillity Zone itself. During each session the background music faded in and out as male and female readers alternated in order to give a balance of voices.

After each session refreshments were served in a separate part of the building and our guests were invited to record their thoughts in a Comments Book. The comments were both moving and reassuring, leading to the hope that other such events would be organized in the future.

In total, 36 guests, six of them 'at-risk' youth from the Bentilee neighbourhood, attended one or more of the themes at the Zone. Many of them were community leaders, others had merely been out shopping and had just popped in out of curiosity. Members of the regeneration team attended, as did disaffected youth from the project who came from homes that had known little of life other than a culture of violence and crime.

The whole event was a collaborative effort, supported by Women for Peace (Stafford), the Joint Villages Forum (the community organization of the Bentilee area) and the Crime Concern 'Mentoring Plus' Project.

Here are some of the comments left in the Comments Book:

'What a marvellous experience. The effort put in by the North Staffs Bahá'ís was great. The room looks fantastic.'

'A peaceful environment created – mesmerised by candle-light – 23 weeks pregnant + and the baby didn't stop moving throughout – effective choice of music.'

'It is difficult to come out of such a peaceful feeling. When you first walk into the Zone you do not notice the water feature, it all comes alive as you let the music, the words enter your soul.'

'Many thanks for a truly beautiful experience which was truly peaceful! Loved the environment, the plants, candles, water and drapes – didn't recognize the place. Thank you.'

'A lovely experience worth coming. Thanks.'

'A totally wonderful experience.'

'What a transformation of the room – beautiful. The energy felt really strong and it felt easy to drift off inside and hear the words float through my consciousness. Thank you very much.'

'An experience I never thought I would feel, it is really wonderful feeling. [A Bahá'í] has made a great difference to all the people he has made contact with. Hope it carries on with their lives.'

'What a great way to spend a Saturday. Thank you for inviting me and for all your hard work in making it such a lovely day.'

'It was very nice to reach the depths of peacefulness that was achieved here today. The words of wisdom are also very useful in our hectic modern world.'

'Something I should and could do more often.'

'Thank you! What a great experience . . . who'd have thought it in the middle of Bentilee! Nice one! Thank you all.'

'How nice to be in a different world. If only.'

'So nice so peaceful, I don't know if I slept but it was wonderful. Thank you.'

'It was wonderful to be on the other side, to relax and be fed instead of giving out as I do when I take the leader's role in meditation. Very peaceful, great environment, the mood was created and worked well, change plainness into an enchanted mist. Thank you everyone.'

'I thought it was very unusual, but it was very . . .' (comment finished here)

'I thought it was wonderful and it was really chill for us.'

'I thought it was very relaxing and very chillin. Yes I would do it again because it was very chillin. I'd also come again for a cup of tea and a biscuit. That was really nice of them to give us free cups of tea.'

Devotionals on Special Occasions

Remembrance
Val McGinley

During the 1980s we lost four babies before birth. It had been my intention for a long time to hold a special devotional meeting to pray for these babes. However, it was only in the mid 90s that I was able to go about planning such a special event. I had mentioned it to a friend who had had a similar experience and she asked if she could 'be included' in the evening. From there the whole thing took off and it grew and grew . . .

The date was fixed and I explained to friends the purpose of this devotional event. The friends began to ask that some of their family members and friends also be prayed for. So I rang friends throughout Ireland – particularly friends who are not Bahá'ís – and invited them to give names of those for whom they wished prayers. I explained the belief that the souls in the next life need us to pray for their progress and told them that all the names would be read out and printed in the devotional booklet. They were also told that the devotional programme would be sent to anyone who would not be able to attend on the night. The response was absolutely wonderful and we knew we had touched something very fundamental and precious to everybody. The list was quite long.

For the devotional evening itself we bought lots of flowers and did the hall and living room up very beautifully. My husband chose special music and we printed out a programme for the readers. The prayers and readings had been sent to them so that they would be familiar with the words. Because of the idea behind this evening I was extremely tense, wondering if it would evoke emotions I would not be able to handle.

The programme was printed on the most beautiful paper I could get – what else but the very best for the word of God! The people for whom we were praying were divided into groups: our babies, children, youth, friends, peers, relatives and parents. Each list of names was read, followed by music and then some readings. I was very aware that because of the connection being made here in this physical plane among these souls that there would also be a corresponding connection made in the realms of God. This brought and brings great comfort to my heart as I imagine these souls 'meeting' for the first time and watching their loved ones praying and listening to the words of the Manifestation of God.

The prayers and readings printed in the programme were attributed either to Bahá'u'lláh or to 'Bahá'í Scripture'. As many non-Bahá'ís were going to read these booklets I did not wish to confuse them with two many names. They would not initially understand about the Báb and 'Abdu'l-Bahá.

The whole evening was very beautiful and uplifting, much to my wonderment. No one got upset even though it was a very emotive evening for some people who had only named babies for the first time for this occasion. During the tea time there was much laughter. There was such a specialness about this event which delighted everyone present.

The booklets were sent off to everyone who had submitted names, as promised, and the response to them was wonderful. People told me years later that they still had this booklet and that it was precious to them for many reasons. One Bahá'í had loaned the booklet to a neighbour whose son had been killed in a car crash. The mother loved the readings so much that she took a quote from the Bahá'í writings and had it inscribed on her son's headstone. The Bahá'í – who had her son's name on the prayer list as he had died as a baby – told me how hard it had been for her to part with the devotional programme booklet, so I gave her another copy.

This evening was such a success that some years later we held another one to pray especially for our parents, whether alive or in the Abhá Kingdom. We followed the same format and again the response was very touching. Friends from Israel, the United Kingdom, Poland, France and many other countries asked that their parents be remembered on this evening and again I thought of the spiritual connections being made in the realms of God. Again the booklet of writings and prayers was sent to everyone. There are many people who have the word of God because of these events.

The memorial evenings went down so well that we did the same event at our Irish Summer School. The friends were told several days in advance and a special book was bought in which people could write the names of their loved ones for the remembrance devotional. Hundreds of names were entered, with people dashing up at the eleventh hour asking to please allow them to write in someone else remembered. The devotional was held but the names were not read out until after the prayers so that anyone who wanted could leave. The atmosphere was very powerful! The two readers of the names told me afterwards that I should have prepared them for the power that would build up as the names were read out. They were both very affected by what had happened.

During a visit to the Scottish Summer School I suggested such a memorial to the organizers who asked if I would arrange it. I did, with the name-readers, prayer-readers and singing and music. On the day I was very ill with a migraine but decided to go as I thought it might look strange if I had been the driving force and then was absent. So I attended, feeling very sick. But as I sat there and heard the names of people I did not know being read out and I listened to the music and prayers, I again was so overcome with such a feeling of light upon light – and a special feeling in the room which I believe was elicited by the evocation of the souls in the Abhá Kingdom. Most of us sat there afterwards lost in our own hearts and thoughts.

Our experience is that these themed devotionals are a very powerful way to get people to connect with prayers and the writings. For people who have a spiritual belief, the idea of a memorial for our loved ones who have passed on is very attractive.

Prayer Vigil
Anne Maund

Following the terrorist attacks in America, the Spiritual Assembly of the Bahá'ís of Chester wanted to offer a prayer meeting to the public. The friends decided to hold a Peace Vigil in the Riḍván Garden created by a Bahá'í living in nearby Childer Thornton.

The local paper must have been intrigued because this time they printed our press release! After the devastation of the cities in the USA, natural simplicity seemed more appealing than ever. Part of the press release read: 'This humble spot on the Wirral Way footpath is dedicated to paradise on earth. Herbert has turned a rough patch of meadowland into a special place with flowers and a stream.'

On Saturday, September 22, friends and guests arrived at dusk and set about illuminating the scene with candles and lanterns . . . By nightfall, as around 25 souls huddled together, each holding a lighted candle, prayers and readings from the Bahá'í, Christian, Hindu, Jewish and Muslim faiths were offered and there was time for silent contemplation.

Afterwards people sipped on hot drinks and quietly chatted, glad that they had expressed their own hopes of peace for mankind.

First published in *Bahá'í Journal UK*, November/December 2001, p. 25. Reprinted with the permission of the National Spiritual Assembly of the Bahá'ís of the United Kingdom.

Tranquillity for Business People
Marga van Luijtelaar-Martens

The European Bahá'í Business Forum (EBBF) is a Bahá'í-inspired association of people who are active or interested in business and management and who are familiar with the Bahá'í ethical and social teachings. It provides a forum in which its members can explore ways of applying those teachings to issues arising out of business and management activities. The EBBF promotes a set of core values vital to business including the application of spiritual principles to economic problems, ethical business practices, recognition that business has a social responsibility as well as an economic mission, steward-ship of the earth's resources and advocacy of sustainable development, the partnership of women and men in all endeavours, the need for a new paradigm of work and consultative decision-making.

Every year the Dutch branch of EBBF is asked to par-ticipate in the 'Motivation at Work' conference in The Hague which is attended by about 700 executives, man-aging directors and human resource managers. The EBBF's offering to the event is a Tranquillity Zone.

The Tranquillity Zone is set up in the middle of the conference facility so that everyone passes it. It is designed to resemble a tent such as Bahá'u'lláh might have used, with Persian carpets, roses and rose water. Sofas and 19 leather armchairs are placed around the sides of the 'tent' and several small tables are set with books about various religions. A large table holds the holy books of the world's religions; next to each holy book a small candle burns. Beautiful, meditative music is played and the atmosphere is serene, simple and radiates beauty.

Whenever enough people are in the room, a ten-minute meditative programme begins. People are welcomed, then a prayer is said in Dutch, a prayer is chanted in Persian and a passage from the scriptures is read in English or Bulgarian, a different one being chosen each time.

Over 125 people visited the Tranquillity Zone on the last occasion, some more than once. Many took away a sheet containing the words of Bahá'u'lláh. A number of visitors indicated that this was a very special experience for them and afterwards called or emailed the conference organizer to tell him how much they enjoyed the Tranquillity Zone. A government ministry official wrote, '(I) was again very much enchanted with the Tranquillity Zone, as I was the first time. The way the Bahá'ís manage to bridge the different religions and create peace and tranquillity in the midst of all the hectic activity on such a day is fantastic.' Another person said, 'This is the most productive hour I have ever spent in my entire life.'

The conference organizer presented all the Tranquillity Zone workers with a bronze figure inscribed with the words 'Thank you so much for your inspiring contribution to Motivation at Work' and remarked that he sees the Tranquillity Zone as one of the pillars of the conference.

Celebration of a New Life
Semira Manaseki and Ian Holland

When by the grace of God a new life arrives into this world, how should we befittingly and publicly celebrate the occasion? After all, what is a new life? And what is our duty as parents? We hold the baby bundle in trust as a blessing from the Almighty and nurture, care and watch over the little one, day by day. For us, the parents of Rodan and Daryon Holland, we decided to host an event to mark the outset of their lives.

Our quandary was exactly how we should celebrate this precious and sacred gift with all our friends and family. After much consultation, we decided to try to craft an event to which we could invite as many people as we knew to be close enough to appreciate our joy and wonder. We wanted to focus the energies, prayers and thoughts of all on our little boys in the hope that they might in some way be guided and protected from the earliest days of their lives in a loving and supportive environment.

We tried to design an occasion where the spiritual mingled with the joys of feasting and gathering with close relatives and friends. We wanted to be able to invoke an atmosphere in which we could take time to reflect on the purpose of life. The two special days that we held for our children were very similar and revolved around two activities. The first was a formal programme of a devotional nature with prayers, music, poems and readings rehearsed by a selection of friends. The second was a social feast. In reaction, many who attended the former, whether religious or not, were moved to tears by the combination of the effect of the atmosphere, the readings, the dignity and the joy they felt. This was especially the case for parents of young children who also had the opportunity to reflect on the wonder of their own good fortune of being gifted with their own 'little miracles'.

A serious amount of planning and organizing went into making the events a success, more so the first time than the second, since second time around we felt like we knew what we were doing. The events shared common features.

SETTING

We intended to invite a large number of guests (around 100), so our home was out of the question. Therefore, we needed to find a venue that combined reverence, beauty and serenity, as well as one in which we could enjoy social high spirits. We also had the additional challenge of keeping the costs down.

We selected a large conservatory room in a local hotel furnished with beautiful floor to ceiling draped curtains arranged in a country style. A small side room opened directly into the main conservatory, which was ideal for parents of babies and toddlers. They could listen to the proceedings from this auxiliary room but not at the expense of distracting others with their playful children – this worked well. As it turned out, such a room proved crucial since at that stage in our lives with all the friend-ships generated from antenatal classes and playgroups, many of our guests had young, somewhat boisterous, children.

The conservatory room, which we booked for both occasions, also had an appealing outlook over the Staffordshire canal, teaming with swans and ducks. We reserved the room for two hours. For Rodan's celebra-tion, we arranged the chairs 'theatre style' and for Daryon we chose a less formal, 'cafe style' with chairs arranged around tables placed about the room. Each table was decorated with a small bouquet of flowers and a place for readers was created, adorned with flowers and microphone, from where a number of our guests stood and read their pieces in view of our audience.

INVITATION

Since this was essentially an event about a baby, we engaged the help of a friend with graphic skills to sketch out for us a 'Winnie the Pooh map' which animated in cartoon-style the location of the hotel in relation to our home.

THE BABY

On the first occasion, the baby whose beginning of life we were celebrating was Rodan Na'im. At the time he was a little over nine months old. On the second occasion baby Daryon Vahid was just under the nine months. The period between the birth and the celebration allowed us time to recover from the turmoils of the baby's arrival, to hold the event in a better season in the year and to plan a befitting ceremony. Also, babies tend to be slightly less demanding or delicate at this age. On both occasions, in the course of the general introductions and welcomes, the babies were introduced to the guests, after which they proceeded to sleep through most of the programme.

THE FORMAL PROGRAMME

At the start of each programme, daddy was given the pleasure of welcoming the guests. He explained that we were Bahá'ís, that Bahá'ís do not have baptism or other equivalent ceremonies and that this event was our idea as proud parents of the newly-arrived little babes. After the baby was formally introduced, the content of the programme was outlined.

The experience of our wedding demonstrated that all of our friends, whether Bahá'ís or not, are moved by various scriptural and poetic readings combined with music. Our 'celebration of life' devotional programmes were mostly a simultaneous combination of readings or prayers with backing music. From the introduction until the end of the devotional part of the programme was about 50 minutes.

For each occasion we selected around 15 prayers or

readings. Approximately half were derived from the Bahá'í writings and the remainder from other religious or literary pieces. We chose one reading on the theme of love from our wedding programme and included it in both celebrations for the boys, thereby connecting the three main celebrations in our family. We also chose around ten pieces of music for each programme. The music was either between readings, which were read with no background music, or were used as background music as the piece was being read.

For the latter group of readers, a copy of the music was provided in advance to help them become familiar with and to rehearse their readings. All readers, with a few exceptions, were given their readings in advance of the day to ensure that they each had the chance to practice. This was an especially useful tactic for those who dread the idea of stepping up to a microphone in front of a small ocean of people. One of Ian's colleagues composed a poem upon the birth of each baby in honour of the little one and this was recited as part of the programme. We were deeply moved by this gesture and by observing the way some of our friends and family had practised the readings and read with such reverence and dignity.

We chose readers who, at the time, had contributed much to supporting us both before and after the arrival of each baby. We also asked people we felt would appreciate and feel in their hearts the passages they were to read. There was a real mix. In the end it turned out that most were not Bahá'ís. Others represented for us great examples of parents. For Daryon's celebration, we also asked Rodan, who was at the time three years and two months old, to say a prayer by heart, which he did. Another Bahá'í child also said a prayer.

SOCIALIZING AND REFRESHMENTS

While waiting for guests to arrive, the hotel served hot and cold drinks. This provided an opportunity for some socializing and for long-distance travellers and others to sensitize themselves to the event. For a short time after the programme, guests enjoyed the hotel's gardens, then gradually drove to our home a couple of miles away and spent the rest of the afternoon and a good part of the evening celebrating with us.

We were grateful to all who made these two beautiful occasions joyous and memorable for us. We will be forever thankful for the bounty of being parents to these two little cherubs whose start of life we celebrated in a fashion which we hope befits the station of these two noble and special young souls.

Appendix 1

Memorandum on Devotional Meetings

Memorandum

To: The Universal House of Justice
From: Research Department
Date: 19 September 2001

Definition and Scope of 'Devotional Meetings'

The Research Department has studied the questions concerning the concept of the devotional meeting raised by Mr . . . in his email of 4 August 2001 to the Universal House of Justice. Mr . . . mentions a recent meeting called by the Local Spiritual Assembly of . . . in which representatives of the Bahá'í institutions who are resident in . . . participated. He reports that one important area of consultation was the devotional meeting. In light of this gathering, Mr . . . enquires whether the Universal House of Justice has specified in any detail 'what a Devotional Meeting looks like'. He is particularly interested in 'the definition and scope of such a meeting'. We provide the following response.

As to the nature of the devotional meetings referred to in recent letters of the House of Justice, in response to a similar question raised by one of the believers, the House of Justice in a letter dated 13 March 2001 written on its behalf, provided the following general guidance:

> Regarding your email message dated 14 February 2001, which has . . . been received at the World Centre, questions concerning local devotional meetings should be referred to your Local or National Spiritual Assembly.

While the Research Department has, to date, been unable to locate any comprehensive definition of the nature and scope of devotional meetings, we have assembled, for Mr . . .'s information and study, a short compilation entitled 'Selected Guidance Concerning Devotional Gatherings'. The compilation consists of extracts from letters written by and on behalf of the Universal House of Justice. A number of themes emerge from perusal of the extracts contained therein. For example:

- Care should be taken to avoid developing rigid practices and rituals (extracts 1 and 6).

- Bahá'ís are encouraged to use the revealed prayers of Bahá'u'lláh and the Báb as well as those of 'Abdu'l-Bahá. It is permissible to have prayers and readings from the Sacred Scriptures of other religions (extracts 2 and 7).

- The form of programme would appear to depend in part on the setting, the occasion, and the purposes of the gathering (extracts 6 and 7).

- The practice of collective worship is one important ingredient in the flourishing of community life. It also reinforces individual spiritual development (extracts 3, 4, and 5).

Given Mr . . .'s interest in the subject of devotional meetings, it is suggested that he might find it helpful to refer to the general compilation entitled 'Prayer, Meditation, and the Devotional Attitude', which was compiled some time ago by the Research Department, and published by a number of Bahá'í publishing trusts. The compilation is also included in 'Compilation of Compilations' (Maryborough, Victoria: Bahá'í Publications Australia, 1991), volume II.

Selected Guidance Concerning Devotional Gatherings

Extracts from Letters Written by and on Behalf of the Universal House of Justice

When one is praying in private, one may do what one's heart prompts in such matters. However when prayers are read at meetings, care should be taken not to develop rigid practices and rituals. (8 April 1982, written on behalf of the Universal House of Justice to an individual believer)[1]

Bahá'ís have the bounty of having the prayers revealed by the Manifestations of God, the Báb and Bahá'u'lláh, as well as by 'Abdu'l-Bahá, which guide us in our devotions, but there is no prohibition of the reading of prayers or selections from the Sacred Writings of other religions. However, the Guardian stated, 'It would be wiser for the Bahá'ís to use the meditations given by Bahá'u'lláh and not use any set form of meditation given by someone else.' (14 September 1982, written on behalf of the Universal House of Justice to an individual believer) [2]

. . . the flourishing of the community, especially at the local level, demands a significant enhancement in patterns of behaviour: those patterns by which the collective expression of the virtues of the individual members and the functioning of the Spiritual Assembly are manifest in the unity and fellowship of the community and the dynamism of its activity and growth. This calls for the integration of the component elements – adults, youth and children – in spiritual, social, educational and administrative activities; and their engagement in local plans of teaching and development. It implies a collective will and sense of purpose to perpetuate the Spiritual Assembly through annual elections. It involves the practice of collective worship of God. Hence, it is essential to the spiritual life of the community that the friends hold regular devotional meetings in local Bahá'í centres, where available, or elsewhere, including the homes of believers. (Riḍván 1996, from the Universal House of Justice to the Bahá'ís of the World) [3]

The spiritual growth generated by individual devotions is reinforced by loving association among the friends in every locality, by worship as a community and by service to the Faith and to one's fellow human beings. These communal aspects of the godly life relate to the law of the Mashriqu'l-Adhkár which appears in the Kitáb-i-Aqdas. Although the time has not come for the building of local Mashriqu'l-Adhkárs, the holding of regular meetings for worship open to all and the involvement of Bahá'í communities in projects

of humanitarian service are expressions of this element of
Bahá'í life and a further step in the implementation of the
Law of God. (28 December 1999, from the Universal House
of Justice to the Bahá'ís of the World) [4]

In the increased capacity of individuals to teach the Faith,
as shown in the thrust of individual initiatives; in the
improved ability of Spiritual Assemblies, Councils and
committees to guide the endeavours of the friends; in the
introduction of new patterns of thought and action which
influenced the collective behaviour of the local community
– in all such respects the system of training institutes
demonstrated its indispensability as an engine of the
process of entry by troops . . . Concurrent with these kinds
of developments, the members of our worldwide community also gave more attention to drawing on the power
of prayer, to meditating on the sacred Word, and to deriv-
ing the spiritual benefits of participation in devotional
gatherings. It is through the workings of these elements of
an intensified individual and collective transformation that
the size of the community is increasing. Although the
number of new believers has as yet only slightly surpassed
those of recent years, it is immensely gratifying to see that
this increase is now geographically widespread, is engaging ever-larger segments of the community, and is
successful in integrating new declarants into the life of the
Cause . . .

The use of the arts became an important feature in the
proclamation, teaching, deepening and devotional activities
of the worldwide community. (Riḍván 2000, from the
Universal House of Justice to the Bahá'ís of the World) [5]

The House of Justice has not prescribed any set forms to be

adopted in a Holy Shrine, whether it be in prayer, meditation or reading of the Holy Scriptures, as long as the
practices followed do not disturb the devotions of others
who are in the Shrine. It does not favour the adoption of the
practice of songs being sung with musical accompaniment
in close proximity to the Shrines. As you can well understand, such singing could well disturb those who, within the
Shrines, are engaged in their devotions.

There are, of course, special occasions, such as the com-
memoration of Holy Days at the Bahá'í World Centre,
when prayers and devotional readings are recited at a gathering held near a Shrine, and the Tablet of Visitation
chanted. A devotional programme, with soloists and orches-
tral accompaniment, is also planned at the entrance to the
Terraces adjoining the Shrine of the Báb, in May 2001. (6
November 2000, written on behalf of the Universal House
of Justice to a Local Spiritual Assembly)[6]

You have asked whether it is permissible for the friends to
recite prayers other than those revealed by the Central
Figures of our Faith, prefacing your query by citing an
instance when a prayer from a different source was chanted
at a Bahá'í public meeting. No prohibition has been found
in the Bahá'í Writings against the recitation at public gatherings of prayers other than those provided in Bahá'í
Scriptures. You are no doubt aware that in devotional programmes at Bahá'í Houses of Worship it is permissible to
include scriptures from other revealed religions, which may
include prayers. You did not specifically mention whether
your concern was about prayers originating from other
sacred scriptures or from compositions by individuals.
Bahá'ís are generally encouraged to use the Creative Word,
including those prayers and Tablets revealed by Bahá'u'lláh,

the Báb and 'Abdu'l-Bahá which are authenticated and published in our Bahá'í literature. A letter dated 8 August 1942, written on behalf of Shoghi Effendi to a National Spiritual Assembly, indicates that while spontaneous prayer is permitted, the revealed verses are preferred because 'the revealed Word is endowed with a power of its own'. The friends, therefore, must use them in their own supplications with radiant joy. This does not mean, however, that in addition to such prayers, they may not, in private, use their own words whenever they feel the inclination to do so. (27 June 2001, written on behalf of the Universal House of Justice to an individual believer)[7]

Appendix 2

Guidance Regarding Seating at Devotional Meetings

Memorandum

To: The Universal House of Justice
From: Research Department
Date: 29 October 2000

Mr . . . requests guidance concerning 'Tranquillity Zones'. According to Mr . . . , there is a growing interest in 'Tranquillity Zones' in many parts of the United Kingdom. A number of Bahá'í communities have participated in this initiative by organizing devotional programmes of readings and music, open to the general public, that are aimed at producing an atmosphere of peace and calm. At such events, it is quite common for the participants to sit on the ground, perhaps on cushions, during the period of devotions.

Mr . . . explains that some of the Bahá'ís have expressed the view that sitting on the ground during devotions is disrespectful, and that the practice should be discontinued. He has been informed that 'while one is praising God or in meditation on the Writings of the

Manifestations of God, one should be sitting on a chair as this is the most respectful act of worship, rather than sitting on the ground, which could imply disrespect'. Mr . . . seeks clarification of this point and enquires whether there are any guidelines on how 'Tranquillity Zones' style meditations and devotions should be observed. We provide the following response:

The Research Department has, to date, not located any general prohibition in the Writings of the Faith concerning sitting on the ground during prayer and meditation. We note, however, that in the Kitáb-i-Aqdas, paragraph 154, Bahá'u'lláh prohibits the 'use of pulpits' and, instead, encourages the use of 'chairs and benches'. Note 168 contains further elucidation of this issue and an explanation of the context in which the guidance applies.

As to whether it is permissible to sit on the floor during prayer, the only reference we have been able to find so far is contained in the following extract from a letter dated 1 April 1982, written on behalf of the Universal House of Justice. The letter specifically addresses the question of the correct position for sitting during the Obligatory Prayer:

Concerning other positions prescribed in the Obligatory Prayers the House of Justice has instructed us to inform you that one of the believers asked the Guardian a question about the correct position for sitting. From the context it seems clear that this question is related to the medium Prayer, but this is not explicitly stated. The Guardian's reply states that sitting on a chair is permissible, but to sit on the floor is preferable and more fitting.

With regard to Mr . . .'s request for guidelines concerning the conduct of 'Tranquillity Zone' type devotional meetings, it is suggested that he seek advice from his National Spiritual Assembly. The National Assembly is in the position to guide him as to what is acceptable and dignified practice in the United Kingdom.[1]

Appendix 3

A Sample Devotional Programme
The Seven Valleys – *The Valley of Love*

1. Music: O Son of Justice!

2. The Valley of Love, from *The Seven Valley*s, Bahá'u'lláh (Bahá'í)

   Music: From Barber's Adagio for Strings

3. From Farid ud-Din Attar, *The Conference of the Birds* (Islam)

   Music: From Mozart's Piano Concerto no. 23

4. From the words of 'Abdu'l-Bahá (Bahá'í)

   Music: From Fauré's In Paradisum

5. Dhammapada 1:1–5 (Buddhist)

   Music: From Beethoven's Moonlight Sonata

6. 1 John 4:7–12, 16–21 (Christian)

   Music: From Pachelbel's Canon and Gigue in C Major

7. Bhagavad Gita 9: 25–9 (Hindu)

   Music: From Tavener's Song for Athene

8. 1 Corinthians 13:1–13 (Christian)

   Music: From Elgar's Nimrod

9. Srimad Bhagavatam 11:8 and from Sri Ramakrishna (Hindu)

   Music: From Massenet's Meditation

10. From the *Hidden Words of Bahá'u'lláh* (Bahá'í)

   Music: From Debussy's *Clair de Lune*

Selection 1

Whither can a lover go but to the land of his beloved? and what seeker findeth rest away from his heart's desire? To the true lover reunion is life, and separation is death. His breast is void of patience and his heart hath no peace. A myriad lives he would forsake to hasten to the abode of his beloved.

From the *Hidden Words of Bahá'u'lláh*

Selection 2
Valley of Love

And if, by the help of God, he findeth on this journey a trace of the traceless Friend, and inhaleth the fragrance of the long-lost Joseph from the heavenly messenger, he shall straightway step into the Valley of Love and be dissolved in the fire of love. In this city the heaven of ecstasy is upraised and the world-illuming sun of yearning shineth, and the fire of love is ablaze; and when the fire of love is ablaze, it burneth to ashes the harvest of reason.

Now is the traveller unaware of himself, and of aught besides himself. He seeth neither ignorance nor knowledge, neither doubt nor certitude; he knoweth not the

morn of guidance from the night of error. He fleeth both
from unbelief and faith, and deadly poison is a balm to him.
Wherefore Aṭṭár saith:

> For the infidel, error – for the faithful, faith;
> For Aṭṭár's heart, an atom of Thy pain.

The steed of this Valley is pain; and if there be no pain this
journey will never end. In this station the lover hath no
thought save the Beloved, and seeketh no refuge save the
Friend. At every moment he offereth a hundred lives in the
path of the Loved One, at every step he throweth a thousand heads at the feet of the Beloved.

O My Brother! Until thou enter the Egypt of love, thou
shalt never come to the Joseph of the Beauty of the Friend;
and until, like Jacob, thou forsake thine outward eyes, thou
shalt never open the eye of thine inward being; and until
thou burn with the fire of love, thou shalt never commune
with the Lover of Longing.

A lover feareth nothing and no harm can come nigh him:
Thou seest him chill in the fire and dry in the sea.

> A lover is he who is chill in hell fire;
> A knower is he who is dry in the sea.

Love accepteth no existence and wisheth no life: He seeth
life in death, and in shame seeketh glory. To merit the mad-
ness of love, man must abound in sanity; to merit the bonds
of the Friend, he must be full of spirit. Blessed the neck that
is caught in His noose, happy the head that falleth on the
dust in the pathway of His love. Wherefore, O friend, give

up thy self that thou mayest find the Peerless One, pass by this mortal earth that thou mayest seek a home in the nest of heaven. Be as naught, if thou wouldst kindle the fire of being and be fit for the pathway of love.

> Love seizeth not upon a living soul,
> The falcon preyeth not on a dead mouse.

Love setteth a world aflame at every turn, and he wasteth every land where he carrieth his banner. Being hath no existence in his kingdom; the wise wield no command within his realm. The leviathan of love swalloweth the master of reason and destroyeth the lord of knowledge. He drinketh the seven seas, but his heart's thirst is still unquenched, and he saith, 'Is there yet any more?' He shunneth himself and draweth away from all on earth.

> Love's a stranger to earth and heaven too;
> In him are lunacies seventy-and-two.

He hath bound a myriad victims in his fetters, wounded a myriad wise men with his arrow. Know that every redness in the world is from his anger, and every paleness in men's cheeks is from his poison. He yieldeth no remedy but death, he walketh not save in the valley of the shadow; yet sweeter than honey is his venom on the lover's lips, and fairer his destruction in the seeker's eyes than a hundred thousand lives.

Wherefore must the veils of the satanic self be burned away at the fire of love, that the spirit may be purified and cleansed and thus may know the station of the Lord of the Worlds.

> Kindle the fire of love and burn away all things,
> Then set thy foot into the land of the lovers.

And if, confirmed by the Creator, the lover escapes from the claws of the eagle of love, he will enter the Valley of Knowledge and come out of doubt into certitude, and turn from the darkness of illusion to the guiding light of the fear of God.   Bahá'u'lláh, *Seven Valleys*, pp. 7–11

Selection 3

From The Conference of the Birds

Love's valley is the next, and here desire
Will plunge the pilgrim into seas of fire,
Until his very being is enflamed
And those whom fire rejects turn back ashamed.
The lover is a man who flares and burns,
Whose face is fevered, who in frenzy learns,
Who knows no prudence, who will gladly send
A hundred worlds towards their blazing end,
Who knows of neither faith nor blasphemy,
Who has no time for doubt or certainty,
To who both good and evil are the same,
And who is neither, but a living flame.
But you! Lukewarm in all you say or do,
Backsliding, weak – O, no, this is not you!
True lovers give up everything they own
To steal one moment with the Friend alone –
They make no vague, procrastinating vow,
But risk their livelihood and risk it now.
Until their hearts are burnt, how can they flee
From their desire's incessant misery?
They are the falcon when it flies distressed
In circles, searching for its absent nest –
They are the fish cast up upon the land
That seeks the sea and shudders on the sand.

Love here is fire; its thick smoke clouds the head –
When love has come the intellect has fled;
It cannot tutor love, and all its care
Supplies no remedy for love's despair.
If you could seek the unseen you would find
Love's home, which is not reason or the mind,
And love's intoxication tumbles down
The world's designs for glory and renown –
If you could penetrate their passing show
And see the world's wild atoms, you would know
That reason's eyes will never glimpse one spark
Of shining love to mitigate the dark.
Love leads whoever starts along our Way;
The noblest how to love and must obey –
But you, unwilling both to love and tread
The pilgrim's path, you might as well be dead!
The lover chafes, impatient to depart,
And longs to sacrifice his life and heart.

Farid ud-Din Attar, *The Conference of the Birds*, pp. 172–3

Selection 4
Words of 'Abdu'l-Bahá

Know thou of a certainty that Love is the secret of God's
holy Dispensation, the manifestation of the All-Merciful, the
fountain of spiritual outpourings. Love is heaven's kindly
light, the Holy Spirit's eternal breath that vivifieth the
human soul. Love is the cause of God's revelation unto man,
the vital bond inherent, in accordance with the divine creation, in the realities of things. Love is the one means that
ensureth true felicity both in this world and the next. Love is
the light that guideth in darkness, the living link that uniteth
God with man, that assureth the progress of every illumined

soul. Love is the most great law that ruleth this mighty and heavenly cycle, the unique power that bindeth together the divers elements of this material world, the supreme magnetic force that directeth the movements of the spheres in the celestial realms. Love revealeth with unfailing and limitless power the mysteries latent in the universe. Love is the spirit of life unto the adorned body of mankind, the establisher of true civilization in this mortal world, and the shedder of imperishable glory upon every high-aiming race and nation.

'Abdu'l-Bahá, *Selections*, p. 27

Selection 5
From the Dhammapada

What we are today comes from our thoughts of yesterday, and our present thoughts build our life of tomorrow: our life is the creation of our mind.

If a man speaks or acts with an impure mind, suffering follows him as the wheel of the cart follows the beast that draws the cart.

What we are today comes from our thoughts of yesterday, and our present thoughts build our life of tomorrow: our life is the creation of our mind.

If a man speaks or acts with a pure mind, joy follows him as his own shadow.

'He insulted me, he hurt me, he defeated me, he robbed me.' Those who think such thoughts will not be free from hate.

'He insulted me, he hurt me, he defeated me, he robbed me.'
Those who think not such thoughts will be free from hate.

For hate is not conquered by hate; hate is conquered by love.
This is the eternal law.

                                        Dhammapada 1:1–5

Selection 6
First Epistle of John 4

Beloved, let us love one another: for love is of God; and
every one that loveth is born of God, and knoweth God. He
that loveth not knoweth not God; for God is love. In this was
manifested the love of God toward us, because that God
sent his only begotten Son into the world, that we might live
through him. Herein is love, not that we loved God, but that
he loved us, and sent his Son [to be] the propitiation for our
sins. Beloved, if God so loved us, we ought also to love one
another.

No man hath seen God at any time. If we love one
another, God dwelleth in us, and his love is perfected in us.
And we have known and believed the love that God hath
to us. God is love; and he that dwelleth in love dwelleth in
God, and God in him. Herein is our love made perfect,
that we may have boldness in the day of judgement:
because as he is, so are we in this world. There is no fear
in love; but perfect love casteth out fear: because fear hath
torment. He that feareth is not made perfect in love. We
love him, because he first loved us. If a man say, I love
God, and hateth his brother, he is a liar: for he that loveth
not his brother whom he hath seen, how can he love God
whom he hath not seen? And this commandment have we

from him, That he who loveth God love his brother also.

First Epistle of John 4:7–12, 16–21

Selection 7
From the Bhagavad Gita

And whoso loveth Me cometh to Me.
Whoso shall offer Me in faith and love
A leaf, a flower, a fruit, water poured forth,
That offering I accept, lovingly made
With pious will. Whate'er thou doest, Prince!
Eating or sacrificing, giving gifts,
Praying or fasting, let it all be done
For Me, as Mine. So shalt thou free thyself
From Karmabandh, the chain which holdeth men
To good and evil issue, so shalt come
Safe unto Me – when thou art quit of flesh –
By faith and abdication joined to Me!

I am alike for all! I know not hate, I know not favour!
What is made is Mine!
But them that worship Me with love, I love;
They are in Me, and I in them!

Bhagavad Gita 9: 25–9

Selection 8
First Epistle to the Corinthians 13

If I may speak in the tongues of men and of angels, but
have not love, I am a noisy gong or a clanging cymbal.
And if I have prophetic powers, and understand all mysteries and all knowledge, and if I have all faith, so as to

remove mountains, but have not love, I am nothing. If I give away all I have, and if I deliver my body to be burned, but have not love, I gain nothing. Love is patient and kind; love is not jealous or boastful; it is not arrogant or rude. Love does not insist on its own way; it is not irritable or resentful; it does not rejoice in wrong, but rejoices in the right. Love bears all things, believes all things, hopes all things, endures all things.

Love never ends; as for prophecies, they will pass away; as for tongues, they shall cease; as for knowledge, it will pass away. For our knowledge is imperfect and our prophecy is imperfect; but when the perfect comes, then the imperfect will pass away. When I was a child, I spoke like a child, I thought like a child, I reasoned like a child; when I became a man, I gave up childish ways. For now we see in a mirror dimly, but then face to face. Now I know in part; then I shall understand fully. So faith, hope, love abide, these three; but the greatest of these is love.

First Epistle to the Corinthians 13:1–13

Selection 9
From Srimad Bhagavatam

Many are the means described for the attainment of the highest good, such as love, performance of duty, self-control, truthfulness, sacrifices, gifts, austerity, charity, vows, observance of moral precepts. I could name more. But of all I could name, verily love is the highest: love and devotion that make one forgetful of everything else, love that unites the lover with me. What ineffable joy does one find through love of me, the blissful self! Once that joy is realized, all earthly pleasures fade into nothingness.

Srimad Bhagavatam 11:8

From Sri Ramakrishna

A disciple asked his master, 'Sir, please tell me how I can see God.'

'Come with me,' said the guru, 'and I shall show you how.'

He took the disciple to a lake, and both of them got in the water. Suddenly the teacher pressed the disciple's head under the water. After a few moments he released him and the disciple raised his head and stood up.

The guru asked him, 'How did you feel?'

The disciple said, 'Oh! I thought I should die; I was panting for breath.'

The teacher said, 'When you feel like that for God, then you will know you haven't long to wait for His vision.'

From Sri Ramakrishna

Selection 10
From the Hidden Words of Bahá'u'lláh

O Son of Man! Veiled in My immemorial being and in the ancient eternity of My essence, I knew My love for thee; therefore I created thee, have engraved on thee Mine image and revealed to thee My beauty.

O Son of Man! I loved thy creation, hence I created thee. Wherefore, do thou love Me, that I may name thy name and fill thy soul with the spirit of life.

O Son of Being! Love Me, that I may love thee. If thou lovest Me not, My love can in no wise reach thee. Know this, O servant.

Bahá'u'lláh, Hidden Words, Arabic 3–5

Bibliography

'Abdu'l-Bahá. *Memorials of the Faithful*. Wilmette, IL: Bahá'í Publishing Trust, 1971.
— *Paris Talks*. London: Bahá'í Publishing Trust, 1967.
— *The Promulgation of Universal Peace*. Wilmette, IL: Bahá'í Publishing Trust, 1982.
— *Selections from the Writings of 'Abdu'l-Bahá*. Haifa: Bahá'í World Centre, 1978.
— *Tablets of Abdul-Baha Abbas*. New York: Bahá'í Publishing Committee, vol. 3, 1930.

Attar, Farid ud-Din. *The Conference of the Birds*. London: Penguin Books, 1988.

Bahá'í Prayers: A Selection of Prayers revealed by Bahá'u'lláh, the Báb and 'Abdu'l-Bahá. Wilmette, IL: Bahá'í Publishing Trust, 2002.

Bahá'í World Faith. Wilmette, IL: Bahá'í Publishing Trust, 2nd edn. 1976.

Bahá'u'lláh. *Epistle to the Son of the Wolf*. Wilmette, IL: Bahá'í Publishing Trust, 1988.
— *Gleanings from the Writings of Bahá'u'lláh*. Wilmette, IL: Bahá'í Publishing Trust, 1983.
— *The Hidden Words*. Wilmette, IL: Bahá'í Publishing Trust, 1990.
— *The Kitáb-i-Aqdas*. Haifa: Bahá'í World Centre, 1992.

— *The Seven Valleys and the Four Valleys*. Wilmette, IL: Bahá'í
    Publishing Trust, 1991.
— *Tablets of Bahá'u'lláh*. Wilmette, IL: Bahá'í Publishing
    Trust, 1988.

Brownstein, Ted. *The Interfaith Prayer Book*. Bloomington, IN:
Special Ideas, 2001.

The Compilation of Compilations. Prepared by the Universal
House of Justice 1963–1990. 2 vols. [Sydney]: Bahá'í
Publications Australia, 1991.

Directives from the Guardian. Compiled by Gertrude Garrida.
New Delhi: Bahá'í Publishing Trust, 1973.

Gail, Marzieh. *Summon Up Remembrance*. Oxford: George
Ronald, 1987.

Hatcher, John S. and Amrollah Hemmat. *The Poetry of
Ṭáhirih*. Oxford: George Ronald, 2002.

Holy Bible. King James Version. London: Collins, 1839.

International Teaching Centre. 'Building Momentum: A
Coherent Approach to Growth', April 2003.
— 'The Spiritual Education of Children and Junior Youth:
    Bahá'í Classes for Children', July 2000.

Lights of Guidance: A Bahá'í Reference File. Compiled by Helen
Hornby. New Delhi: Bahá'í Publishing Trust, 5th edn. 1997.

Momen, Wendi. *A Basic Bahá'í Dictionary*. Oxford: George
Ronald, 1989.

Nabíl-i-A'ẓam. *The Dawn-Breakers: Nabíl's Narrative of the Early*

Days of the Bahá'í Revelation. Wilmette, IL: Bahá'í Publishing Trust, 1970.

The Peace Bible: Words from the Great Traditions. Compiled and edited by Steven Scholl, with an foreword by Hans Küng. Los Angeles, CA: Kalimát Press, 2nd edn. 2002.

Rabbaní, Rúḥíyyih. *The Priceless Pearl*. London: Bahá'í Publishing Trust, 1969.

Scholl, Steven. 'The Remembrance of God: A Sufi invocation technique in Bábí and Bahá'í scriptures', manuscript.

Scriptures of the World. CD. Chandigarth, India: Computers International.

Seekers' Prayers: A Gift of Prayers and Selected Bahá'í Writings. Bloomington, IN: Special Ideas, 1995.

Shoghi Effendi. *The Advent of Divine Justice*. Wilmette, IL: Bahá'í Publishing Trust, 1990.
— *Arohanui: Letters of Shoghi Effendi to New Zealand*. Suva, Fiji: Bahá'í Publishing Trust, 1982.
— *Bahá'í Administration*. Wilmette, IL: Bahá'í Publishing Trust, 1968.
— *God Passes By*. Wilmette, IL: Bahá'í Publishing Trust, rev. edn. 1974.
— *High Endeavors: Messages to Alaska*. [Anchorage]: National Spiritual Assembly of the Bahá'ís of Alaska, 1976.
— *The Promised Day is Come*. Wilmette, IL: Bahá'í Publishing Trust, rev. edn. 1980.
— *The World Order of Bahá'u'lláh*. Wilmette, IL: Bahá'í Publishing Trust, 1991.

The Universal House of Justice. *The Four Year Plan*. Riviera Beach, Florida: Palabra Publications, 1996.

— Letter of the Universal House of Justice to the Bahá'ís of the World, Riḍván 1996.
— Letter of the Universal House of Justice to the Bahá'ís of the World, Riḍván 1998.
— Letter of the Universal House of Justice to the Bahá'ís of the World, 26 November 1999.
— Letter of the Universal House of Justice to the Bahá'ís of the World, 28 December 1999.
— Letter of the Universal House of Justice to the Bahá'ís of the World, Riḍván 2000.
— Letter of the Universal House of Justice to the Bahá'ís of the World, Riḍván 2001.
— Letter of the Universal House of Justice to the Bahá'ís of the World, 10 January 2002.
— Letter of the Universal House of Justice to the Bahá'ís of the World, 17 January 2003.
— Letter of the Universal House of Justice to the Bahá'ís of the World, Riḍván 2003.
— Letter of the Universal House of Justice to the Conference of the Continental Boards of Counsellors, 26 December 1995.
— Letter of the Universal House of Justice to the Conference of the Continental Board of Counsellors, 9 January 2001.
— Letter of the Universal House of Justice to National Spiritual Assemblies, 25 February 1986.
— Letter written on behalf of the Universal House of Justice to an individual, 8 April 1982.
— Letter written on behalf of the Universal House of Justice to an individual, 14 September 1982.
— Letter written on behalf of the Universal House of Justice to an individual, 27 June 2001.
— Letter written on behalf of the Universal House of Justice to the National Spiritual Assembly of Norway, 1 September 1983.

— Memorandum of the Research Department to the Universal House of Justice, 29 October 2000.
— Memorandum of the Research Department to the Universal House of Justice, 19 September 2001.
— Message of the Universal House of Justice to the Dublin Conference, 2 June 1982.
— *Messages from the Universal House of Justice 1963-1986: The Third Epoch of the Formative Age.* Wilmette, IL: Bahá'í Publishing Trust, 1996.
— *Wellspring of Guidance.* Wilmette, IL: Bahá'í Publishing Trust, 1976.

A World of Faith: World Celebration Special Edition. Salt Lake City: Interfaith Council of Salt Lake City, Utah, 2002.

References

Introduction

1. From a letter of the Universal House of Justice to the Conference of the Continental Boards of Counsellors, 9 January 2001.
2. International Teaching Centre. 'Building Momentum: A Coherent Approach to Growth', April 2003.
3. From a letter of the Universal House of Justice to the Bahá'ís of the World, 17 January 2003.
4. International Teaching Centre. 'Building Momentum: A Coherent Approach to Growth', April 2003.

Chapter 1: The Devotional Life

1. From a letter written on behalf of Shoghi Effendi to an individual, 8 December 1935.
2. 'O people of the earth! Living in seclusion or practising asceticism is not acceptable in the presence of God.' Bahá'u'lláh, *Tablets*, p. 71. 'O concourse of monks! Seclude not yourselves in your churches and cloisters. Come ye out of them by My leave, and busy, then, yourselves with what will profit you and others. Thus commandeth you He Who is the Lord of the Day of Reckoning.' Bahá'u'lláh, *Epistle to the Son of the Wolf*, p. 49.
3. Bahá'u'lláh, *Gleanings*, p. 276.
4. 'O people of Bahá! It is incumbent upon each one of you to engage in some occupation – such as a craft, a trade or the like. We have exalted your engagement in

such work to the rank of worship of the one true God.'
Bahá'u'lláh, *Kitáb-i-Aqdas*, para. 33.

5. Bahá'u'lláh, *Epistle to the Son of the Wolf*, p. 49.

6. 'Conservation of the Earth's Resources', in *Compilation*, vol. 1, pp. 78–9.

7. Scholl, 'The Remembrance of God', manuscript, p. 2.

8. Bahá'u'lláh, *Kitáb-i-Aqdas*, para. 149.

9. From a letter written on behalf of Shoghi Effendi to an individual, 15 May 1944, in *Lights of Guidance*, p. 456.

10. Shoghi Effendi, *Bahá'í Administration*, pp. 185–6.

11. 'Abdu'l-Bahá, in *Compilation*, vol. 1, p. 377.

12. From a letter of the Universal House of Justice to all National Spiritual Assemblies, 27 March 1978, in *Lights of Guidance*, p. 326.

13. From a letter written on behalf of the Universal House of Justice to a European National Spiritual Assembly, 1 September 1983.

14. From a letter of the Universal House of Justice to the Bahá'ís of the World, 28 December 1999.

15. Bahá'u'lláh, *Kitáb-i-Aqdas*, para. 18.

16. From a letter of the Universal House of Justice to the Bahá'ís of the World, 28 December 1999.

17. ibid.

18. From a letter written on behalf of the Universal House of Justice to a European National Spiritual Assembly, 1 September 1983.

19. From a letter of the Universal House of Justice to National Spiritual Assemblies, 25 February 1986.

20. From the message of the Universal House of Justice to the Dublin Conference, 2 June 1982.

21. Shoghi Effendi, *Promised Day is Come*, p. 123.

22. Shoghi Effendi, *World Order*, p. 162.

23. From the message of the Universal House of Justice to the Dublin Conference, 2 June 1982.

24. From a letter written on behalf of the Universal House

of Justice to a European National Spiritual Assembly, 1 September 1983.

25. From the message of the Universal House of Justice to the Dublin Conference, 2 June 1982.

26. 'Abdu'l-Bahá, *Tablets*, vol. 3, p. 631.

Chapter 2: The Devotional Life of the Bahá'í Community

1. In 'Questions and Answers' in the *Kitáb-i-Aqdas*, Bahá'u'lláh explains: 'Although the words "at the hour of dawn" are used in the Book of God, it is acceptable to God at the earliest dawn of day, between dawn and sunrise, or even up to two hours after sunrise.' Question 15, p. 111.

2. Bahá'u'lláh, *Kitáb-i-Aqdas*, para. 115.

3. Shoghi Effendi, *God Passes By*, p. 340.

4. Bahá'u'lláh, *Kitáb-i-Aqdas*, Notes, p. 190.

5. ibid.

6. Bahá'u'lláh, *Kitáb-i-Aqdas*, para. 31.

7. Momen, *Basic Bahá'í Dictionary*, pp. 149–50. See 'Abdu'l-Bahá, *Selections*, pp. 93–5.

8. 'Abdu'l-Bahá, *Selections*, pp. 93–4.

9. From a letter written on behalf of the Universal House of Justice to the National Spiritual Assembly of Brazil, 8 May 1984, in *Lights of Guidance*, p. 555.

10. ibid.

11. ibid.

12. ibid.

13. 'Abdu'l-Bahá, *Selections*, p. 94.

14. Bahá'u'lláh, in *Compilation*, vol. 2, p. 228.

15. From the letter of the Universal House of Justice to the Bahá'ís of the World, Naw-Rúz 1974, in *Messages from the Universal House of Justice 1963–1986*, p. 269.

16. From a letter of the Universal House of Justice to all National Spiritual Assemblies, 25 May 1975, in ibid. p. 311.

17. 'Abdu'l-Bahá, *Bahá'í World Faith*, p. 411.
18. From the letter of the Universal House of Justice to the Bahá'ís of the World, Riḍván 1996.
19. From a letter of the Universal House of Justice to the Bahá'ís of the World, 28 December 1999.
20. From a letter of the Universal House of Justice to the Conference of the Continental Boards of Counsellors, 9 January 2001.
21. From a letter written on behalf of Shoghi Effendi to an individual, 13 August 1936, in *Lights of Guidance*, p. 475.

Chapter 3: What is a Devotional Meeting?

1. Bahá'u'lláh, in *Compilation*, vol. 1, p. 188.
2. 'Abdu'l-Bahá, in ibid. p. 195.
3. From a letter written on behalf of Shoghi Effendi to an individual, 4 February 1950, in *Compilation*, vol. 2, p. 315.
4. 'Abdu'l-Bahá, *Selections*, p. 94.
5. From a letter of the Universal House of Justice to the Conference of the Continental Boards of Counsellors, 9 January 2001.
6. From a letter of the Universal House of Justice to all National Spiritual Assemblies, 25 June 1967, in *Wellspring of Guidance*, p. 116.
7. Shoghi Effendi, *Directives from the Guardian*, p. 70–1.
8. From a letter written on behalf of Shoghi Effendi to the National Spiritual Assembly of the United States, 11 April 1947, in *Lights of Guidance*, p. 607.
9. From a letter written on behalf of Shoghi Effendi to the National Spiritual Assembly of the United States and Canada, 2 April 1931, in ibid. p. 607.
10. From a letter written on behalf of the Universal House of Justice to an individual, 7 June 1974, in ibid. p. 457.
11. Memorandum of the Research Department to the Universal House of Justice, 19 September 2001.

Chapter 4: Planning Devotional Meetings

1. Letter of the Universal House of Justice to the Bahá'ís of the World, 17 January 2003.
2. International Teaching Centre, 'Building Momentum: A Coherent Approach to Growth', April 2003.
3. Shoghi Effendi, *High Endeavors*, p. 70.
4. Letter of the Universal House of Justice to the Bahá'ís of the World, 17 January 2003.
5. Words of 'Abdu'l-Bahá to Mrs Mary L. Lucas, as quoted in *A Brief Account of My Visit to Acca*, Chicago: Baha'i Publishing Society, 1905, pp. 11–14, in *Compilation*, vol. 2, p. 78.
6. From a letter written on behalf of the Universal House of Justice to an individual, 8 April 1982.
7. From a letter written on behalf of the Universal House of Justice to an individual, 14 September 1982.
8. From a letter written on behalf of the Universal House of Justice to an individual, 27 June 2001.
9. From a letter written on behalf of Shoghi Effendi to an individual, 15 June 1935, in *Lights of Guidance*, p. 460.
10. From a letter of the Universal House of Justice to the National Spiritual Assembly of the United States, 13 March 1964, in *Compilation*, vol. 1, p. 12.
11. From a letter written on behalf of the Universal House of Justice to an individual, 6 February 1975, in *Lights of Guidance*, p. 460.
12. Bahá'u'lláh, *Kitáb-i-Aqdas*, para. 149.
13. Bahá'u'lláh, in *Compilation*, vol. 1, p. 188.
14. ibid.
15. Bahá'u'lláh, *Gleanings*, p. 7.
16. From a letter of the Universal House of Justice to the National Spiritual Assembly of Australia, 6 February 1973, in *Lights of Guidance*, p. 411.
17. From a letter written on behalf of the Universal House of Justice to an individual, 1 August 1983, in *Compilation*, vol. 1, p. 457.

18. From a letter written on behalf of the Universal House of Justice to an individual, 8 May 1979, in ibid. p. 54.

Chapter 5: Music and Arts

1. Bahá'u'lláh, in *Compilation*, vol. 1, p. 1.
2. Bahá'u'lláh, *Gleanings*, p. 141.
3. 'Abdu'l-Bahá, *Paris Talks*, p. 176.
4. 'Abdu'l-Bahá, *Bahá'í World Faith*, p. 377.
5. Bahá'u'lláh, *Tablets*, p. 72.
6. 'Abdu'l-Bahá, *Paris Talks*, p. 175.
7. Bahá'u'lláh, *Epistle to the Son of the Wolf*, p. 26.
8. 'Abdu'l-Bahá, *Promulgation*, p. 52.
9. 'Abdu'l-Bahá, in *Lights of Guidance*, p. 410.
10. Bahá'u'lláh, *Kitáb-i-Aqdas*, para. 51.
11. 'Abdu'l-Bahá, from 'Table Talk', Acca, July 1909, in *Compilation*, vol. 2, pp. 76–7.
12. From letter written on behalf of Shoghi Effendi to an individual, 15 November 1932, in *Lights of Guidance*, p. 413.
13. 'Abdu'l-Bahá, *Selections*, p. 112.
14. 'Abdu'l-Bahá's words to Mrs Mary L. Lucas, as quoted in 'A Brief Account of My Visit to Acca', 1905, in *Compilation*, vol. 2, p. 79.
15. ibid.
16. 'Abdu'l-Bahá, in *Bahá'í World Faith*, p. 378.
17. From a letter of the Universal House of Justice to the National Spiritual Assembly of Guyana, Surinam and French Guiana, 22 February 1971, in *Compilation*, vol. 1, p. 450.
18. From a letter of the Universal House of Justice to the National Spiritual Assembly of Australia, 6 February 1973, in *Lights of Guidance*, p. 411.
19. From a letter written on behalf of Shoghi Effendi to an individual, 7 April 1935, in *Compilation*, vol. 2, p. 81.
20. From a letter written on behalf of Shoghi Effendi to the

National Spiritual Assembly of the United States and Canada, 2 April 1931, in *Lights of Guidance*, p. 607.

21. From a letter of the Universal House of Justice to the National Spiritual Assembly of Uganda and Central Africa, 19 August 1965, in *Lights of Guidance*, p. 609.

22. 'Abdu'l-Bahá's words to Mrs Mary L. Lucas, as quoted in 'A Brief Account of My Visit to Acca', 1905, in *Compilation*, vol. 2, p. 78.

23. See Hatcher and Hemmat, *Poetry of Ṭáhirih*.

24. From a letter written on behalf of the Universal House of Justice to an individual, 8 May 1979, in *Compilation*, vol. 1, p. 54.

25. From a letter written on behalf of Shoghi Effendi to the National Spiritual Assembly of the United States and Canada, 20 July 1946, in *Lights of Guidance*, p. 411.

Chapter 6: Hospitality

1. Bahá'u'lláh, in *Bahá'í Prayers*, p. 40.

2. Shoghi Effendi, *Arohanui*, p. 29.

3. From a letter of the Universal House of Justice to the Bahá'ís of the World, 10 January 2002.

4. From a letter written on behalf of Shoghi Effendi to the Bahá'í Inter-Racial Committee of the National Spiritual Assembly of the United States, 27 May 1957, in *Lights of Guidance*, p. 531.

5. 'Abdu'l-Bahá, *Paris Talks*, pp. 15–16.

6. Shoghi Effendi, *Advent of Divine Justice*, p. 34.

7. Gail, *Summon Up Remembrance*, pp. 258–9.

Chapter 7: The Coherence of the Core Activities

1. From the letter of the Universal House of Justice to the Bahá'ís of the World, Riḍván 2001.

2. From the letter of the Universal House of Justice to the Conference of the Continental Boards of Counsellors, 26 December 1995.